EMS and the Law
A Legal Handbook for EMS Personnel

Arnold S. Goldstein

D0094267

Robert J. Brady Co.
A Prentice-Hall Publishing and
Communications Company

Bowie, MD 20715

EMS and the Law: A Legal Handbook for EMS Personnel

Library of Congress Cataloging in Publication Data

Goldstein, Arnold S.
    EMS and the law.

    Includes index.
        1. Medical personnel—Malpractice—United States.
    2. Emergency medical personnel—Legal status, laws, etc.—United
    States.   I. Title.   II. Title: E.M.S. and the law.
    KF2905.3.G64 1983   346.7303'32   83-2560
    ISBN 0-89393-423-1   347.306332
    ISBN 0-89303-422-3 (pbk.)

Prentice-Hall International, Inc., London
Prentice-Hall Canada, Inc., Scarborough, Ontario
Prentice Hall of Australia, Pty., Ltd., Sydney
Prentice-Hall of India Private Limited, New Delhi
Prentice-Hall of Japan, Inc., Tokyo
Prentice-Hall of Southeast Asia Pte. Ltd., Singapore
Whitehall Books, Limited, Petone, New Zealand
Editora Prentice-Hall Do Brasil LTDA., Rio de Janeiro

Printed in the United States of America

83 84 85 86 87 88 89 90 91 92 93   10 9 8 7 6 5 4 3 2 1

Executive Editor: Jim Yvorra
Production Editor/Text Designer: Michael J. Rogers
Art Director/Cover Design: Don Sellers
Typesetting by: Harper Graphics, Waldorf, MD
Indexer: Leah Kramer
Typefaces: Melior (text) and Friz Quadrata (display)
Printed by: Fairfield Graphics, Fairfield, PA

CONTENTS

PREFACE

The possibility of liability affects every health care provider—including Emergency Medical Technicians, Paramedics, and even First Responders rendering assistance to the ill or injured.

As an increasing trend, this possibility of liability has had a dramatic impact on how care is provided, the risks practitioners are willing to accept, and even the cost. It is that fear of the lawsuit, and the apparent willingness of more and more patients to file it, that requires all providers understand how malpractice claims arise, and then to take a long hard look at their own mode of practice with the objective of reducing liability, while providing the patient with the care he or she is entitled to.

Most people associate the term "liability" or "malpractice" with physicians. It is not, however, a problem only of concern to the medical profession. In reality the problem extends to every member of the health care team as they are all potential defendants once a malpractice claim arises. With ever-increasing frequency, other health professionals are being held accountable as targets of patients turned plaintiff. And unquestionably the initiator of emergency medical care—the First Responder, Paramedic, and EMT—will have their actions evaluated with increased scrutiny.

That's what this book is designed to accomplish. It will be more than a presentation of the law. It will be an effective guide highlighting specific problems, procedures and even trends that can create liability for the emergency care provider. The most important feature of this book are the clear, concise, and practical steps you can take to reduce or avoid that liability.

As an emergency care provider, I assume you have little or no prior legal training. In fact, this may be your first "in-depth" exposure to the law of your profession. With this in mind, I present the legal principles in simplified, easy-to-understand language. Legal terminology is kept to an absolute minimum. To assist you with those few unavoidable legal terms not otherwise defined within the text, I have included a comprehensive legal glossary to refer to.

The law stated in the narrative can be confusing. To clarify it I have extensively used short case problems to illustrate the application of the law to a practice setting. These cases not only bring the law to life, but aid you in deciding how you might handle the same situation in your daily work. Many of the case examples will test your newly acquired knowledge by having you provide the likely conclusion.

As you proceed through the book, you will find an increased ability to apply the abstract legal principles not only to the cases I present, but more importantly, to the hundreds of situations you encounter in your work.

For this book to have its greatest value it has to provide you not only with the general theories applicable to all malpractice actions, but moreover it must give you the specific and precise guidance for conducting yourself within your profession. This book contains that careful blend of the general theory of liability with the practical "how to do it" information you will need.

You will find a discussion on all the contemporary problems of emergency care, including the expanded obligations mandated by recent court decisions, governmental regulations, and the development of new technology and procedures used in the field. As with the rapidly changing state of the arts—and law—affecting all health practitioners, the emergency care specialist must react not only to the present but also to the future. As these mutational changes bring about new responsibility they also present new legal issues. Hopefully, this book will accurately predict those future trends and adequately forecast their legal implications.

This book focuses on the First Responder, Paramedic and Emergency Medical Technicians (EMTs). Its scope is necessarily confined to the legal aspects of patient care to the point where hospitalization or physician involvement begins. Clearly, the responsibilities of each may differ; however, the legal principles will apply to all in a large extent. By using this book physicians and nurses involved with an Emergency Department can gain useful information on the legal principles guiding emergency care providers before them, and the principles that can extend even to their own practice.

I have presented law seminars to emergency care providers throughout the country. From these seminars I have been able to pick out the most common questions asked. You will find these questions, and my own opinion, as to the most likely legal conclusion at the end of the book.

Let me provide a caveat. Law like medicine deals in probabilities and seldom absolutes. Many questions defy a certain answer because providing that ultimate answer or decision is the function of the court. To render that decision may require more facts than can be provided in this or any other book. Further, a legal outcome will depend somewhat on the applicable law within a particular state together with all the factual and subtle legal variables that make each case stand alone. This is what makes law so mystical to the layman and perhaps so fascinating to the lawyer.

Faced with a specific legal problem you must rely on the advice of your own counsel. Only he or she can intelligently assess all the facts, apply the laws of your state, and give you the guidance and protection you need. No book can serve as his or her substitute.

It is my hope that when you complete this book you will have a firm understanding of how liability arises—where you may encounter it—and how you can avoid it. With that newly gained perspective you will be able to do what you were meant to do: provide the best possible emergency medical care.

Arnold S. Goldstein

ABOUT THE AUTHOR

Arnold S. Goldstein is a practicing attorney with 20 years experience in the field of medical malpractice and emergency care law.

As a senior partner in the Boston law firm of Meyers, Goldstein & Chyten, the author represents numerous ambulance service corporations in the State of Massachusetts and has lectured before many professional and governmental groups on the topic of emergency care and health law.

His articles on health law and malpractice have appeared in many national publications including *Modern Nursing Home, Drug Topics, The Apothecary, Pharmacists Management Journal,* and *American Druggist.*

Mr. Goldstein holds the degrees Bachelor of Science in Pharmaceutics, Master of Business Administration, Doctor of Jurisprudence, and Master of Laws. He is a member of the Massachusetts and Federal Bars and also holds a full professorship at Northeastern University where he conducts courses in medical and health law.

Dedicated to my wife
Marlene
for both her encouragement to write this book
and her tireless efforts in assisting me in its preparation.

1

EXPANDING LIABILITY OF THE EMERGENCY CARE PROVIDER

At a recent law seminar conducted for a group of EMTs one participant asked an interesting question—just what are the odds of being sued for malpractice? Unfortunately I had no ready answer; however, the question demanded an answer, if only to put into perspective the importance of liability avoidance for the typical EMT.

Several weeks later, after consultation with three major insurance companies extending malpractice coverage to ambulance services, I had my answer. Statistically there will be about one claim filed for every 50,000 patient trips. At first glance that would appear to present a very remote likelihood of a lawsuit. However, if you take this same statistic and relate it to your own chances of facing a malpractice suit during your career, the statistic translates into an average of one or perhaps two malpractice suits during a lifetime activity as an emergency care provider.

This figure only represents a statistical average. Many EMTs will never experience the malpractice problem, and others will be forced to defend their actions in court several times.

The disclosure of these statistics is not intended to cause alarm or even to imply that the risks inherent in emergency medical care are disproportionate to the rewards. Compared to other health professionals the emergency care provider has a substantially reduced chance of being sued. Physicians and even dentists, for example, will reportedly be involved in litigation, with one out of every 20,000 patients within the next decade.

Unquestionably the likelihood of adverse litigation will increase for all health practitioners in the next two decades if the future continues the present trend. This is one reason why the legal aspects of medical care is an increasingly important component of patient care and why health providers are radically changing their approaches to providing that patient care. As more than one writer has termed it, "defensive medicine" may well be the wave of the future.

1

What a health care professional does—or refuses to do—for a patient will be influenced by the law. Some may even argue that the legal consequences will be more than an influencing factor: they may become the controlling factor.

To what extent legal considerations will influence or control your approach to emergency medical care will depend on your awareness of the malpractice problem, and the importance you attach to it. Regardless of your present outlook of the malpractice problem, it will eventually change as you react to the increased dominance of the law as a part of emergency medical care.

WHY MALPRACTICE CASES ARE ON THE INCREASE

Several years ago faculty members at Columbia University conducted an intensive study to define the reasons for the malpractice explosion. Alarmed by a 400 percent surge in claims over a ten-year period, the study had important legal, medical, and sociological consequences. Here is a summary of the findings:

1. Increased malpractice claims against health care providers reflected the general trend of increased litigation in all areas of law. We are becoming a highly litigous society. If we were to look at litigation over commercial transactions, contracts, corporate matters, or even real estate disputes we would see corresponding, if not equal, increases. People are turning to the courts with increasing frequency. Malpractice cases may be on the crest of that wave but they are still part of that wave. General litigation has doubled in the 1970's compared to the decade of the 1960's. However, in the same time period malpractice cases increased four-fold. Why then have malpractice cases increased twice as rapidly as other forms of litigation?

2. Restructuring of the health care industry is a partial answer to the increase of malpractice suits. The Columbia University study reasoned that as medical care became less personalized through the opening of clinics, health maintenance organizations, referrals to specialists, and other cost and medically efficient methods, the long standing personal relationship between the patient and provider evaporated. Patients are reluctant to sue a practitioner that they have had a long-standing relationship with. That reluctance does not exist with a practitioner offering limited or short-term involvement. Clearly, this is one characteristic that works against emergency medical care. By its very nature this care defies either a long-term or continuous relationship. An EMT or paramedic will be judged by an assessment

of his or her performance, and a less than favorable assessment cannot be neutralized by personal relationships.

3. Highly publicized malpractice awards act as a fuel for other claims. No other type of legal recovery gets this type of publicity, and few avenues of litigation offer the average person the actual—or imagined—opportunity for a higher award than a malpractice claim. Many patients look at the malpractice claim as the "pot of gold," although most claims are either dismissed or result in awards or settlements of less than 10,000 dollars. Undoubtedly, emergency care providers become "targets" like other health practitioners when patients seek high, but usually deceptive, judgments.

4. Changes in medicine partially explain the dramatic increases in malpractice suits. New technology, expanding or shifting responsibilities, and therapeutic agents of increased toxicity all present inherent risks. These very changes also alter the patient's perception of what he or she might expect as reasonable results, and when those results are not achieved litigation may be the end product. Very few areas of medical care have experienced the changes that have affected emergency medical care.

5. The government plays an important role in the malpractice explosion. New laws and regulations issued by administrative and licensing agencies carefully and increasingly define and mandate standards of practice. A violation of a regulation can highlight negligent conduct. Recently enacted regulations involving emergency medical care represent necessary safeguards for the patient but at the same time set forth characteristics of practice that cannot be breached.

6. The legal community itself is a contributing factor. In past years many negligence lawyers would discourage malpractice because they were busy litigating automobile cases. The rise of "no fault" auto insurance sharply curtailed the number of cases involving adversary litigation. Therefore, many negligence lawyers faced with this loss of income suddenly turned to medical malpractice and product liability cases as new areas of involvement. Cases that were previously discouraged or turned down were being picked up for legal representation.

Are there other and lesser reasons for the malpractice phenomena? Certainly. But what is clear is that health care practitioners are not being increasingly sued because they are increasingly negligent. In fact, most of the evidence holds to the contrary. Health care has never operated at a higher level of quality or with practitioners of greater competence. Emergency medical care shares this same increased quality of patient care, but nevertheless will still fall victim to the counter-balancing forces that will continue to cause malpractice cases to grow.

WHO DEFINES THE MALPRACTICE PROBLEM

You can look at the malpractice problem from many angles. To define the problem, you must first decide on a specific focus. Is the focus on the quality of care, cost, administration, availability of care, law, morality, or loss to the patient? Should the concern be the standards to be followed by emergency care providers or the cost to maintain those standards that may be borne by the individual patient, family, community, government, or insurance company? Finally, should we not define the problem from the point of view of the cost to the practitioner both in terms of monetary risk and loss of reputation?

As you can see, each person involved in a malpractice encounter sees a different problem, and each problem is seen differently by the persons involved. Consider the attitudes and perceptions that do exist.

MALPRACTICE—THE PATIENT'S VIEWPOINT

When a person becomes a patient, he or she encounters a whole new set of experiences in a strange environment. This is particularly true in emergency care, for it may be the first time in his or her life that he or she has experienced acute illness or an injury requiring emergency care.

Surrounded by unknown equipment, procedures, and unfamiliar personnel, the emergency care patient does not know what to expect and has little or no prior experience on which to base those expectations. Yet the patient will suppress all reactions in order to reach one goal: the restoration of health. In achieving that end the patient will subconsciously assign to each health practitioner a sphere of responsibility in the process.

Whether an emergency care provider properly performed within his or her sphere of responsibility for the patient will depend not simply on how he or she *did* perform, but equally how the patient believed he or she should perform. In short, the patient may have wrongfully imposed unrealistic standards on the emergency care provider and then held the provider liable when those expectations were not fulfilled.

Of course, thoughts of malpractice only come about when the patient suffers complications or adverse results that he or she believes should not have happened. Once convinced that the problem was created by human error, the attempt to assign responsibility for that error begins.

At this point the patient will begin to trace the involvement of all the health care providers involved. It is also at this point that the performance of the emergency care provider will be measured and assessed.

What does the patient expect when receiving emergency care? The answer to that question will depend on who is providing the care and under what conditions.

First Responders as a category imply personnel who have obtained training from a First Responder course, and can provide assistance under the Emergency Medical Services System (EMS). Typically, these personnel include law enforcement agents, police or fire personnel, or even a co-worker or union representative trained as a First Responder.

Although a First Responder has special training and qualifications, and is an integral part of the EMS system, many patients see their role as that of a "Good Samaritan" or even a "well-intentioned" layman. This outlook does not diminish either the skill or the contribution of the First Responder, both of which are considerable.

Why patients group First Responders with the non-medically trained bystander rendering first aid is due to two factors: first, most patients are simply not aware of the role of the First Responder. They seldom are aware that the policeman or co-worker rendering aid is highly qualified under a specific training program. The second reason is that First Responders are not looked upon as being part of the medical establishment. Both legislatively and in practice, nothing can be further from the truth, but consider if from the viewpoint of the patient. A fireman hardly resembles a "health practitioner." A truck driver with First Responder qualifications does not send a bill. Indeed, what the First Responder appears to resemble is the "well-intentioned" layman rather than a person trained as an important first link in the health care process.

Considering this outlook, most patients are reluctant to assign responsibility to First Responders. The First Responders' involvement is limited in terms of time and the degree of aid rendered. All First Responders know that the assistance rendered in those first few moments may be all-important; nevertheless, unless error specifically points to the First Responder, few patients believe the injury or illness underwent needless aggravation at the embryonic stage.

From a psychological viewpoint, most patients are extremely grateful for the assistance of the First Responder. It's the First Responder who was first on the scene and alleviated mental trauma if not physical pain as well. Cloaked with the appearance of a "Good Samaritan," most patients find it psychologically or morally conflicting to sue for anything less than obvious and serious error on the First Responder's part.

Legal defenses also serve to insulate the First Responder from liability. In many states the First Responder will be protected by the "Good Samaritan" statutes. First Responders who are part of police or fire departments, or work for other governmental agencies, will be largely protected by the defense of governmental immunity. These legal defenses are undoubtedly the third reason for the very few lawsuits filed against the First Responder.

Patients use a different perspective in assessing EMTs. The EMT has the role of a health care provider. Unlike the First Responder where medical assistance may only be a supplement to his or her occupation, the EMT is viewed as being primarily involved in patient care. Moreover, the EMT, particulary one working for a commercial ambulance service, cannot hide behind the appearance of a "well-intentioned" layman. Patients look to the EMT like they would a physician or any other health practitioner. The patient is paying for the EMT's service and they expect the service to be provided properly. For these reasons the EMT increasingly incurs the same malpractice risks facing other health practitioners. The outlook of the EMT has changed in recent years and will continue to change even more in future years as the role of the EMT is altered.

In past years, the EMT was viewed as providing little more than a transport function. In recent years it has become clear that the EMT has the further duty to provide emergency medical care. The public, being increasingly aware that the EMT is the recipient of specialized training, specific legislative and professional standards, and obligations to the patient, finds little difficulty in making the EMT a defendant in litigation.

Emergency departments in hospitals have traditionally been the recipients of adverse litigation. The public never has difficulty in seeing their role as full participants in the medical arena with the reciprocal responsibility.

I point out the differences in how the patient sees the various emergency care providers to erase the thought that each shares the same degree of risk or accountability.

From a strict legal approach, each emergency care provider does have a legal responsibility, and each can be successfully sued if that responsibility is not fulfilled properly. That, however, still does not change the way patients, as potential litigants, view their respective roles and liabilities.

Increased education and public awareness of the actual role of the First Responder and EMT will bring about increased responsibility and a change of those views. Once those views change, what the patient will expect to receive in competency of care will undergo the same change.

Ideas of what to expect from an emergency care provider is only one dimension of the total attitude of the patient considering a malpractice case. Sometimes an emergency care provider will create unjustified expectations or promises for the patient. This, of course, creates "false hopes" and when the end result does not conform with what was promised, the discrepancy can produce disappointment and possibly a lawsuit. It may well be that what the emergency care practitioner promised or represented was totally unrealistic and well beyond the ability of any practitioner to accomplish. This does not change the patient's perception of what *should* have been accomplished in this instance.

The tendency to sue is a highly individualistic trait. Some patients constantly impose unrealistic standards on health practitioners and are quick to sue when those standards are not met—and they seldom are. This is the same type of person who goes through life imagining they have fallen victim to all types of "wrongs" and with this same philosophy sue business associates, landlords, and even their attorneys once their ill-founded lawsuits fail.

Some of these "professional litigators" suffer from emotional problems. Others cling to the belief that every lawsuit has a certain "nuisance" value and even a small settlement justifies the time and effort spent in litigation; that, too, is part of the perception process.

Even geography plays a role. California and other western states statistically have a higher incidence of malpractice cases on a per capita basis. Larger urban areas exceed rural areas on the same per capita assessment. Studies have proven that age, income, religion, sex, and even marital status play a role in molding a patient's outlook—and defining who is likely to sue or not sue.

Given these many variables, it is illogical to assume that a malpractice case will necessarily be the end result of professional malpractice. In many instances unjustified actions are filed and, with equal certainty, many patients with real claims fail to even consider litigation. The connection between a lawsuit or lack of one—and professional liability—is in all too many instances coincidental at best.

MALPRACTICE—THE ATTORNEY'S VIEWPOINT

The attorney represents an extension of the patient so his or her viewpoint will be discussed next.

To a considerable extent the attorney acts either as a "brake" or an "accelerator" for a patient considering a malpractice case. Whether the patient's view of liability is joined by the attorney's is significant in deciding the issue of whether to sue or not.

Many patients believe they have a case against a health practitioner only to find out after legal consultation that either a legal claim does not exist, or that a lawsuit is not practical due to defenses that can be raised or other procedural or legal obstacles.

The factors that influence the attorney's recommendation are per-haps as numerous as those affecting the patient's decision.

As a first step, the attorney must carefully assess the claim to determine whether it has sufficient merit to proceed with a suit. This in turn requires a careful review of the facts and the conclusion that liability does exist as a matter of law.

This process in itself is highly subjective. One problem facing the attorney is that he or she only has the facts as obtained from the client, bolstered perhaps by some medical reports. Nevertheless, the patient's version is only one side of the story, and all too often attorneys find that the practical facts substantially change once the defendants introduce their defenses.

This is one problem with litigation as technical and complex as a modern malpractice claim—the plaintiff's attorney can seldom be certain that the facts as presented by the client are factual until long after a suit is commenced.

Whether the facts, as stated, create liability under some recogniz-able theory of law represent the second part of the malpractice equa-tion. Unless the case presents obvious liability, different attorneys may reach different conclusions over the prospects of winning.

Essentially, the facts weighed against the law must convince the attorney that a case exists. To what extent the "probability" of suc-cessful litigation will be must exist before an attorney will accept the case and will also depend on the attorney. There are some at-torneys that will accept cases with only a slim possibility of success, and others may demand that a case be sufficiently convincing to assure a 70–80 percent likelihood of a favorable verdict.

Even with a case presenting a clear argument for liability, the attorney must consider the provable damages to decide whether it is economical to proceed. For example, a patient may well have a case against an EMT; however, if the award for the injury and dam-ages is small and only worth several thousand dollars or less, then the attorney will most likely discourage the suit.

The reason for discouraging the suit is that it takes virtually the same time and effort to process a small claim case as one with a substantial injury. If the attorney is working on a one-third contingent fee basis, he or she may logically decide it is not worth the time to spend countless hours on a case that may result in a fee of 1,000 dollars or less.

Considering the question of apparent liability with damages—to determine whether a case is worth pursuing—will greatly be influenced by the attorney's own practice.

Well-experienced attorneys with an active trial practice may logically set higher standards on the cases they accept than would newer members of the Bar with less demands on their time. In many instances a patient will consult with two or three attorneys who will decline the case, and finally have the case accepted by an attorney who either sees a possibility with the case not shared by the prior attorneys, or that the case fits into his or her economic requirements. This is a very common occurrence, and certainly even the most questionable cases will eventually be accepted by some attorney, if the client continues to consult with attorneys until an agreeable counsel can be found. In many instances, however, a patient will drop the idea of a suit once an attorney discourages the action.

Some attorneys will accept a questionable case because the patient is a client of long standing. Others may be motivated to accept a case on the hope that this case will bring about a long-standing client relationship. Others may see little economic benefit but may be professionally challenged by an interesting legal point. Still others may hope for a quick settlement, a satisfied client, and a fee corresponding to the time spent on the case.

Increasingly, attorneys must be cautious in accepting a case. If the case is foolish and obviously without merit, the defendant, upon winning the case, can sue both the attorney and his or her client for abuse of the legal process. Several judgments have been entered against attorneys who have prosecuted groundless claims. This is an additional reason why the attorney must always make sure that the claim has some actual basis.

In the final analysis, whether an emergency care provider will be sued, and the extent to which the lawsuit will be prosecuted, always depends on the attorney the patient chooses to talk with.

MALPRACTICE—THE INSURANCE COMPANIES' VIEWPOINT

With increased malpractice litigation resulting in a greater number, and the size, of awards to successful plaintiffs, the insurance underwriters providing malpractice coverage are finding themselves paying out more in benefits each day.

The concept of insurance is not complicated. When you come across a risk you cannot afford to take, you pay the insurance company to take that risk for you. Your premiums (payments) are carefully structured to represent the risk transferred to the insurance company, and enough additional money is added into the premium to cover operating costs and profits.

With increased malpractice claims, insurance companies must pass on the costs in the form of higher premiums to balance the higher costs. Indeed, many insurance companies complain that even with increased premiums, they still operate at a loss. Therefore, insurance underwriters demand one of two alternatives. Underwriters insist that they be allowed to increase their premiums which are already extremely high for certain health practitioners; or that they be allowed to decrease malpractice coverage without decreasing premiums.

Barring the possibility of these two alternatives, many insurance underwriters no longer participate in malpractice coverage, or condition their future participation by requiring that the malpractice problem be decreased through enforced government regulations which control, limit, or reduce the size and number of malpractice awards. These alternative demands are determined solely by economic questions. Profit is the main motive of the insurance industry. The industry is less concerned with the rights and moral liabilities of the parties than with its own profit margins, cash flow, and stock dividends. It is these very demands, however, to which emergency care providers are forced to respond.

Reducing these trends to show their actual impact on emergency care providers, the future will undoubtedly see:

1. Premiums skyrocketing by 20 percent or more each year.

2. Insurance companies imposing higher co-deductables through which the insured health care practitioner would pay a larger percentage of each claim.

3. Refusal by the insurance companies to insure for excessive amounts.

4. Limitations on the coverage offered, excluding "high risk" activities such as CPR and drug administration.

5. An increased trend by EMS providers electing to operate without insurance.

6. Additional training courses for emergency care providers sponsored by insurance companies, which may by required for coverage.

7. Increased demands to reduce malpractice litigation by "screening" boards and the claiming of maximum recovery awards against municipalities and other nonprofit entities.

8. Increased government payments to offset insurance premiums.

9. Higher fees charged by EMTs to cover the increasing cost of insurance.

Finally, the insurance companies will either bring the risk down to the point where it balances with the premiums, or emergency care providers will operate without this necessary protection.

MALPRACTICE—THE FIRST RESPONDER'S VIEWPOINT

First Responders have traditionally treated liability as a possibility but not a probability. This is due in part to the relatively few cases being filed against First Responders, and perhaps of greater consequence, the realization that issues of liability will be handled by the municipality or company employing them.

That being the case, First Responders consider the problem to be one of monetary risk to their employer. Of course, a liability action would be directed equally at the First Responder but in due course most malpractice cases directed against a First Responder are finally paid by the employer.

That does not suggest that First Responders should ignore the problem. It is possible that a First Responder could face monetary loss as an employer may have defenses that could shield the employer but not the employee—such as governmental immunity. At the very least, the First Responder would be required to spend considerable time participating in the defense of his or her own acts.

First Responders will undoubtedly face increased accountability and risk as the public becomes more aware of their role in emergency situations.

Some potential problems facing the First Responder involved in a malpractice claim are the loss of reputation, standing in one's field and, perhaps even the loss of employment.

All health professionals report that the one devastating element of the malpractice suit is not the financial loss—as this is usually handled by the employer or insurance underwriter—but rather its impact on one's "self confidence." Many of these same practitioners report that it has the effect of causing them to re-examine their own methods of practice and to practice "defensively."

There have been First Responders who have found difficulty in obtaining employment in that field after a malpractice suit. Some employers avoid hiring First Responders involved in a malpractice suit on the basis that their insurance costs can increase once they are added to the payroll. Even worse, an insurance company may decline coverage entirely.

Another reason why employers often resist hiring "high risk" employees is that in the event of a later claim, the patient can present the argument that the employer was negligent by not adequately "screening" the qualifications of its employees.

Although most First Responders are employed by municipalities, the municipality is under an equal obligation to assess the rising costs of insurance, or as an alternative, the risks associated with a "self-insurance" mechanism.

Their handling of the problem will require employers to:

1. Increase the standards and qualifications in hiring First Responders.
2. Require continuous training.
3. Make sure that only qualified practitioners perform First Responder services.
4. Define the types of First Responder activities that will be allowed. Many municipalities now have a policy of delaying wherever possible emergency treatments that may properly fall within the scope of the EMT's responsibilities.
5. Transfer more emergency calls to private ambulance services.

Of all the practitioners under an EMS service, it will most likely be the First Responder that undergoes the most significant change relating to the malpractice problem. How a First Responder reacts to the word "malpractice" in 1990 will be somewhat different than his or her reaction in 1980.

MALPRACTICE—THE EMT'S/PARAMEDIC'S VIEWPOINT

Much of what has been said about the First Responder applies equally to the EMT/paramedic. However, there are some differences in their outlook of the problem.

One major distinction exists in the fact that EMTs have already faced a large number of lawsuits making the thought of a malpractice suit an immediate rather than a futuristic concern.

A second distinguishing characteristic is the type and length of care rendered to the patient. Where the First Responder has relatively little contact, the EMT/paramedic's contact is usually longer and more extensive. It can almost be said that although both the First Responder and EMT/paramedic each have their individual responsibilities to the patient, the EMT's relationship is somewhat more structured.

The EMT/paramedic is generally more conscious of the fact that, as with other health providers, his or her activities will be carefully examined in the review of a malpractice claim. The EMT/paramedic is also sensitive to the fact that unlike the First Responder, who is generally protected by the "Good Samaritan" statutes, this protection all too often is not available to the EMT/paramedic.

Another distinguishing feature is that the EMT/paramedic is required to function within a maze of laws and regulations, and the violation of any one can create near-automatic liability.

Perhaps the main concern is the cost of the malpractice problem from the EMT/paramedics, or with greater accuracy, the viewpoint of the private ambulance service. As a privately owned corporation charging a fee, these ambulance services do not have the same defenses available as does a municipality employing a negligent First Responder.

This situation interconnects with the economics of insurance. As insurance costs rise, ambulance services are required to pass these costs on to the patient through higher billings. That, however, is not always possible. Many ambulance services contract with municipalities on a "low bid" basis. In others, reimbursement is fixed under a third-party plan. In either event the ambulance service has a limited opportunity to pass the costs on to the patient.

Faced with this dilemma, more and more ambulance services are reducing insurance costs by limiting coverage or agreeing to a high co-insurance provision. In some instances they "self-insure" and protect themselves by having few assets owned by the operating company.

The financial risk of the EMT/paramedics depends on the ability of their employer to protect them and to pay any malpractice judgment. In many instances that financial capability is lacking given the EMT/paramedics high degree of exposure.

A final problem is the changing role of the EMT/paramedic. New technology and modes of treatment create a responsibility that is new to the industry. Many EMT/paramedics have yet to develop the required skills and familiarity with these procedures. Notwithstanding the accelerating licensure laws and training programs, the fact exists that many EMT/paramedics consider this expanded role to be a new source of liability.

Defensive practice is considerably more noticeable among EMT/paramedics than First Responders. As emergency care continues to grow and the role of all EMS personnel becomes more defined and upgraded, a more rational balance between defensive practice and excellence in patient care will come about. Until then the "malpractice" problem may continue to exist, but it is the patient's welfare that must dictate the level of provided service. Operating with that philosophy may be the one major deterrent to a malpractice suit.

2

LAW AND THE LEGAL PROCESS

For many emergency care providers this book represents their first "in-depth" look at the law. Although law plays an important role in both our personal and professional lives, it can be safely said that the average person has little understanding—not only of the law itself—but how the law works.

Most of the chapters in this book will discuss what lawyers refer to as the "substantive" law, or the legal principles that can create liability in your professional practice. However, to appreciate the substantive law, it is equally important to understand both the sources of law, and the procedures by which legal rights are enforced. That's what this chapter is intended to accomplish.

WHAT IS "LAW?"

Law has been defined in many ways depending on its source. Perhaps the best definition is that law provides enforceable rights between parties. Key to the definition is the word "enforceable." Moral duties, conforming to social customs or "norms," and ethical standards all impose obligations; however, these are distinguished separately from "law" because they are not legally enforceable.

When we use the word "law" we speak only of a situation where a party can seek help through the courts or other groups with enforcement or disciplinary powers.

SOURCES OF LAW

To understand what is meant by "law" it is first necessary to have an awareness of its sources. When we recite what "the law" is on a given subject, we must have some reference point or basis. The reference is the legal source.

These are primary sources of law:

- common law
- statutory law
- regulations
- constitutional law

1.   Common Law

Common law is best known as case law. It is the growth, categorizing, and formation of legal principles through case decisions. Most of our common law can be traced back to the earliest civilizations, notably to Roman Law and in more recent times to English Law. Most of the common law that we rely upon today is a modern application of the law that governed our ancestors thousands of years ago. It is not surprising that this is so because basic human relationships do not change even though surrounding technology may make significant advances.

Even the earliest civilizations needed to recognize and enforce the basic rights between people. These same basic rights and the need to enforce them exists today.

Later in this book we will discuss your liability for treating a patient without his or her consent. This is called "battery." In reality it is only a development on the historical cases creating liability for the "wrongful or unauthorized touching of another."

Negligence is another example of a common law source. Countless cases have defined the elements of a negligence claim to the point where an attorney can recite the law with reasonable legal accuracy. The facts may change from case to case, but the legal principles seldom do.

If we say that common law is in fact the sum total of court rulings on earlier and similar cases, then we should look for a certain degree of change and perhaps even a certain lack of order and clearness. Frequently, attorneys will attempt to interpret legal principles from prior cases to convince a court what the law is—and that it favors his or her client's position. Essentially, that is all a legal brief is. Not surprisingly, opposing counsel will try to find past cases that recite yet other legal holdings favorable to his or her client.

Let's see how this would work in practice. All attorneys accept the legal practice that negligence requires a breach of the "standard of care" owed to the patient. All prior cases are clear on that point. However, suppose an EMT with basic life support training attempts to perform treatment usually performed by Paramedics with advanced life support training. The question then becomes, by which "standard" will the defending EMT be measured?

Different jurisdictions may adopt different rulings. One state may hold that the EMT will be held to the degree of skill of an EMT. Others may hold that the EMT will be held to the standard of the Paramedic. Where this legal issue has not been earlier decided within a state by an appeals court decision, it may be likely that even different trial courts within the same state will not agree.

To add to the problem it is important to note that within the United States there are 50 separate jurisdictions. Within any given state there is one governing common law doctrine on a given point at any one time. The common law operative within a state is usually the most recent ruling on the issue by a state's highest court. As you go through this book you will see my statements on the law qualified to reflect exceptions or different views adopted by some states.

Changes in the common law do happen. Courts can alter or even remove the prior common law with completely different rulings, thus seeming to abandon or reverse the established law created by earlier court rulings. Since the courts create the common law they can change it, although this does not frequently occur.

Common law changes usually result with advances in technology where the existing common law doctrines do not seem to logically apply. In other instances a court may abandon a ruling on the basis that it has no reason for continuing. The marked erosion of common law decisions granting immunity to hospitals and even governmental bodies highlights the shifting philosophy of the courts.

2.   Statutory Law

Unlike common law, statutory (legislative) law is familiar to most people. Most of us are constantly referred to statutory provisions regulating all phases of our lives—from taxes to the legal age for drinking.

Where common law originates from court decisions, statutory law is created by a law-making or legislative body. It may be Congress, a state legislature, or a regulation issued by a Federal or State administrative agency.

Where common law may be difficult to define, particularly where there are conflicting or perhaps no prior cases on point, statutory law is crystal-clear. It precisely states the law.

A further distinction between common law and statutory law is in the area of coverage. Common law deals with the basic or perhaps more fundamental legal issues needed to regulate society. Most statutory law, on the other hand, regulates subtle or complex matters. These matters include the regulation of commerce, industry, professions, taxes, and numerous other areas relating to our existence.

Legislative bodies have broad power to enact any statute providing it bears some reasonable relationship to protecting the health or general welfare of the public. These powers are commonly referred to as "police powers" and are liberally thought of as the authority to regulate.

Statutory law takes precedence over common law. A legislative body through enactment of a statute can overrule what has been a common law precedent. It is only in the absence of a statute that case law decisions will prevail.

In many instances statutory law will not completely override common law but only modify it. For example, negligence is a common law doctrine. There is no statute defining its elements, nevertheless the time period to commence negligence actions is governed by statute. Good Samaritan statutes freeing certain persons from negligence liability is still another example of statutory law overriding the common law doctrine. In still other instances, court decisions created a common law immunity which were eventually ended by statute.

In determining the law, the existence of a statute should first be sought. When there is no statutory coverage, common law decisions should be the guiding factors.

3.   Regulations

A regulation is enacted by an administrative agency to regulate a trade, profession, or area of commerce. To fully understand how regulations work, it is first necessary to understand the functions of administrative agencies.

Administrative agencies exist at both the Federal and State levels. Their functions and procedures are comparable, and only their areas of responsibility change.

When a legislative body enacts a broad body of laws to regulate a profession or activity, it does so recognizing the fact that passage of the laws will not be sufficient alone to make the laws be carried out or enforced.

Therefore, the legislature will create an administrative body and give it three basic powers within a definable area. These powers are:

1. The authority to make regulations.

2. The authority to hold hearings on whether to revoke or suspend licenses or permits issued by it, or to carry out other sanctions for violations of law.

3. The duties to administer the law, which includes the duty to examine, license, maintain records, and enforce the laws under its jurisdiction and otherwise oversee the activities within its area of authority.

A regulation then becomes the delegated right to enact law as passed to the administrative agency from a legislative body. For example, a state legislature may give a Board of Registration in Medicine (a state agency) the authority to regulate medical practice within the state. Granted this authority, the medical board would have the right to enact regulations defining record keeping requirements by emergency care physicians.

Since a regulation is below a statute, it can only exist where no statutory coverage exists, or it can be added to or provide further detail to a statute. A regulation cannot, however, contradict a statute.

Regulations are enacted only by the administrative agency and bypass the legislative process. The steps that must be taken by the agency to enact a regulation are defined by the Administrative Practices Act existing in every state and at the Federal level. Normally the procedure consists of notifying interested parties of the possible enactment of a regulation (including modification or termination of an existing regulation), a public hearing, and filing the certified regulation with the Secretary of State.

Legislative bodies grant the regulation enactment authority to agencies for the following reasons:

1. Legislative bodies do not want to spend their time on laws that are detailed or administrative in nature. For example, Congress provides in the Federal Controlled Substances Act that persons handling dangerous drugs must be registered. However, Congress properly left it to the Drug Enforcement Administration to decide through regulation the procedures on how to register.

2. An agency may have greater technical expertise to enact regulations. A state agency charged with the responsibility to regulate ambulance services may be in a better position to define through regulation mandatory ambulance equipment than could be logically handled by statute.

3. An agency can usually respond quickly to the obvious need for a law than could a legislative body, and where emergency laws are required, an agency may be able to respond in weeks.

A regulation has the full force of law. It's violation can bring about the loss of a license and even criminal proceedings. Emergency care providers should strictly follow all operative regulations because not following regulations can have severe consequences.

Emergency medical providers, as part of a growing profession, have only recently been faced with administrative regulation. Even in these instances, most regulations have dealt with matters of granting licenses, equipment, and ambulance standards. Unlike other health care professions accountable to a specified state agency (medicine, dental medicine, nursing, or pharmacy) EMTs and paramedics are regulated as additional health care providers through a Board of Medicine or Departments of Public Health.

With the realization that EMTs/paramedics are professionals, it can be expected that their activities will increasingly be assigned to new and appropriate state agencies who will enact regulations defining essential standards of practice.

4.   Constitutional Law

The Constitution provides the fourth source of law. The Constitution can guarantee protection against governmental abuse and it is used frequently in this context.

Surprisingly, the rules of the Constitution can even apply to routine emergency medical care. Consider for a moment the following:

- Can the police demand the records of an ambulance service without a warrant or is that a violation of the search and seizure provisions of the Fourth Amendment?

- Can an EMT's license be revoked without giving the EMT a hearing to defend himself, or would that be a deprivation of a "property right" in violation of the "due process" clause of the Fourteenth Amendment?

- Can a state agency draw up regulations barring an ambulance service from sending handbills to sources for referral, or would that be an unlawful violation of the "freedom of speech" provisions of the First Amendment?

- Can a prosecutor force an EMT to give information about a possible violation of law, or is that an abridgment of the EMT's rights against self-incrimination under the Fifth Amendment?

Through these few examples, and perhaps countless other possible examples, you can readily see that the Constitution can apply to your everyday problems—and rights. As you proceed through this book you will see Constitutional references made to the more likely areas of practice.

HOW LAWS INTERRELATE

Unfortunately, "law" does not exist as one "neatly tied" package. It is to some extent an overlapping patchwork flowing from different levels of government and its various agencies. EMS personnel may be forced to operate within a statutory and regulatory maze.

The handling of controlled drugs by emergency care physicians (or paramedics with advanced life support qualifications) is a case in point. These persons would have to comply with:

- Provisions of the Federal "Controlled Substances Act" passed by Congress.

- Provisions of regulations from the Federal Drug Enforcement Administration.

- The State "Controlled Substances Act."

- Regulations by state agencies having jurisdiction over the handling of controlled drugs by EMS personnel.

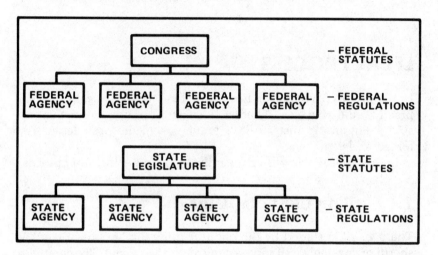

At least four law-making bodies would dictate through their respective statutes and regulations what the physician must and must not do.

Considering the four possible levels of law, the opportunity for conflict does arise. For example, a Federal regulation may say something which is the opposite of a State statute. The practitioner's ability to interpret and adjust to the conflicts are necessary if he or she is to practice in agreement with the law.

Some basic rules and guidelines to remember are:

1. Federal laws (and regulations) always supersede and have priority over state laws. Therefore, a Federal regulation will take precedence over a State statute if there is a question over which law should be followed.

2. Where it is possible to comply with two or more laws simultaneously, but one law is stricter than another, follow the strictest law and you will be conforming with all.

The relationships between laws can be confusing to most people and can even create questions for the court to decide. However, all EMS personnel should:

1. Obtain all Federal and State statutes and regulations concerning emergency medical care.

2. Understand what the respective requirements are.

3. Keep informed about new statutes and regulations affecting their practice.

4. Take an active role as individuals, and through associations, to work for the enactment of future laws that will both aid in professional development and in increased protection of the patient.

LEGAL PROCESS

Hopefully you will never have to defend yourself against a malpractice suit. However, whether it has merit or not, any patient can start a lawsuit against an EMS provider and the provider will be forced to defend.

In this section we will uncover the steps in the litigation process.

1.   Filing the Complaint

The lawsuit is started by the plaintiff filing the lawsuit in court. A sheriff or constable will serve a copy on the defendant. The complaint will say who is involved in the action, the basis for the claim, and the damages or recovery sought.

The complaint may contain several grounds for recovery, each constituting a "cause of action." For example, a patient may accuse an EMT of negligently treating the patient and say the treatment was performed without the consent of the patient. In this instance the patient would sue for:

a. Battery (the treatment without consent)

b. Negligence (error in treatment)

To recover an award under each cause of action, the plaintiff must prove the existence of the necessary elements.

2.   The Defendant's Answer

Upon receipt of the complaint, the defendant will have a fixed number of days to file a defense. Usually this will be in the form of an answer where the defendant either admits or denies each paragraphed accusation of the plaintiff's complaint. The answer would also include any specific or "affirmative" defenses the defendant may have. In this manner the areas of disagreement or contest are known.

Instead of an answer, the defendant may file various motions to dismiss. These motions usually raise a reason as to why the lawsuit should not go forward, such as improper court jurisdiction, statute of limitations, immunity, or prior discharge by reason of a defendant's bankruptcy. If the court agrees, the case will be summarily dismissed; however, upon denial of the motions the defendant will then have to file an answer.

3.   Pre-Trial Discovery

Essential to all litigation is the right to "discover" evidence in possession of the opposing party or some third party. This provides counsel the opportunity to discover the "case" of his or her opponent and avoid surprises at the time of the trial.

Discovery can take several forms:

- *Interrogatories*—a series of written questions to be answered in writing by the opposing side.

- *Depositions*—questions orally presented, and answered, under oath before a court stenographer.

- *Request to produce documents*—require the opposing party to present all documents or other forms of material evidence.

In a well prepared case, there will be little likelihood of surprise at the time of trial. Each side will have had an adequate opportunity to find out everything the opposing side may use in evidence through the discovery process.

4.   Trial on the Merits

The key to the entire legal process is, of course, the trial. Since the plaintiff has to prove the accusations he or she has made, he or she presents his or her case first. During this presentation the defense may cross-examine the plaintiff's witnesses. The situation is then reversed as the defense goes forward. Clearly, it's beyond the scope of this book to search further into the complexities and technicalities in presenting a case; however, most of you have had reasonable exposure to the process even if it is through television and movies.

5.   Appellate Review

After a judgment is entered by the court, either party can take an appeal. The appeal can seek to set aside the entire verdict or an excessive award.

Grounds for appeal are usually limited to errors in law made by the court, as it is not the function of the appeals courts to "double guess" the findings of the jury. Errors of law may involve erroneous rulings on motions, or the use of improper evidence or inaccurate instructions to the jury.

To most people, the procedural steps between the initial interview and the final determination of the case may appear both elementary and orderly. What may be hidden from the eyes of the casual observer are the hours of research, drafting, review of witnesses and evidence, court appearances on motions, correspondence, preparation and the formulation of strategy.

The typical malpractice case can consume thousands of hours, many thousands of dollars in legal fees, and several years to conclude. It can also result in a verdict that can monetarily and professionally destroy the defendant. This is sufficient reason for EMS providers to avoid potential liability.

TEST YOUR KNOWLEDGE

1. How does "substantive" law differ from "procedural" law?
2. List the possible sources of law.
3. Will the common law of one state necessarily be the same in other states?
4. What major areas of legal concern to you as an EMS provider will be governed by common law?
5. How can the common law be changed?
6. Which is considered the higher body of law: common or statutory law?
7. Provide two examples of how statutory law modifies common law applicable to EMS personnel.
8. What is meant by a "regulation?" How does it differ from a statute?
9. What are the typical functions of an administrative agency?
10. Why do legislative bodies give administrative agencies the authority to enact regulations?
11. Which administrative agencies in your state have the authority to control or regulate you as an EMS provider?
12. If there is a conflict between Federal and State Law, which will prevail? Is your answer the same if the State law is more restrictive than the Federal law?
13. On what basis can you appeal a judgment in a malpractice case?

3

UNDERSTANDING THE LAW OF NEGLIGENCE

It is impossible to truly understand the application of malpractice principles without first having a firm understanding about the law of negligence. In practice, most malpractice cases involve negligence. There can be other bases for a lawsuit, such as assault and battery or invasion of privacy which involve claims of a different nature, but these are statistical rarities in the emergency care setting.

Due to the generally large percentage of cases based on negligence, lawyers and most people alike tend to change the term "negligence" for "malpractice." Although every act of professional negligence may be malpractice, it does not necessarily follow that every act of malpractice is negligence.

THE ELEMENTS OF NEGLIGENCE

What is negligence? If a patient alleges that an EMT performed negligent treatment, what should he or she have to prove, and how could he or she prove it?

Negligence can be recognized but few people can adequately define it. You may simply call it "carelessness" or "not doing what is required"; however, in a legal context the term takes on a precise meaning.

Every negligence case requires the plaintiff to prove the existence of these four elements:

1. The defendant had a *duty* to the plaintiff.

2. The defendant breached that duty by not observing the *standard of care* required.

3. The failure of the defendant to comply with the standard was the *cause* of,

4. *Damage* or injury to the plaintiff.

If any element above is missing the plaintiff cannot win the case. That is why it is important to analyze each element carefully to determine whether a sufficient case exists. Reciprocally, EMS personnel must be aware of their obligations to avoid the creation of the negligence claim.

Let's consider each element of the negligence claim in greater detail.

WHEN YOUR DUTY TO ACT BEGINS

Unless you have a duty to act, you cannot be held liable because you failed to act. Interestingly, only Vermont has a statute imposing upon certain health providers the obligation to come to the rescue of those in medical need. Other than the unusual Vermont statute, no other jurisdiction requires a health provider to respond where no legal duty exists otherwise.

As an example, if an EMT employed by a private ambulance service comes upon an accident case while returning from another call, is he liable if he does not stop? On these facts he would not. He was not responding to that accident, and assuming further that he had no contractual obligation to respond to the call, any response would be voluntary. To stress the point, a physician taking a leisurely walk could ignore another pedestrian suffering a heart attack.

We may all agree that this defies moral obligations or even our own outlook on ethical standards. However, neither morality or ethics serve as a substitute for a legally required duty.

Frequently, EMS personnel express concern over the question of when their duty to act does arise. This is an important consideration, for you can be held liable if you do have that duty and ignore it. For these reasons you should clearly understand when a legal duty does arise. Duty may be imposed under any of the following situations.

1.   When You Are Under a Contractual Duty

Relationships between patients and health providers are usually based on a contractual relationship, or the understanding that the provider agrees to render service to the patient.

This "contractual" relationship does not follow a formal procedure. If a patient phones an ambulance service, and the dispatcher confirms that an ambulance will be sent, that will be sufficient to imply the existence of an agreement.

Generally, the test is whether the provider indicates by his or her actions the agreement to accept the patient. The determination is not always easy. Take a patient transported to an Emergency Department. If the patient was left on a stretcher for one hour and then refused admission, would you say the hospital "accepted" the patient? What if the hospital gave the patient a blood transfusion, would that change your conclusion?

Telephone screening by an ambulance service is generally not enough to create a provider-patient relationship, rather it is the process by which the service will decide whether emergency care is required.

The fact that you serviced a patient once does not create the duty to provide care on a new occasion. When you provide emergency care your duties end when the patient is transported to the hospital. Should the patient require future EMS care, you can decline. This may happen where ambulance service was provided months earlier and the patient's bill remains unpaid.

Ambulance services often have contracts with a municipality. Does it follow, then, that the ambulance service will be liable to a patient within that town if service is denied? There is no certain answer to this problem. Some state court decisions hold that the contract is only between the municipality and the ambulance service—and since the patient is only a beneficiary under that contract, he or she does not have sufficient standing to sue, although the municipality may have grounds for a breach of contract. Other states hold that a patient can sue as a beneficiary. Still others may consider whether a municipal contract, by its terms, means acceptance of all calls. If a city has contracts with several services, the obligations of any one ambulance service is diminished if not extinguished.

Ambulance services under municipal contract should have their situation reviewed by counsel to determine the duty they do have. Contracts should also specify whether the service can refuse service to patients, with or without good cause.

First Responders, EMTs and paramedics employed by municipalities face even more troublesome legal problems. Can a town-employed paramedic refuse to respond to a real call for emergency care? Virtually all cases hold that a municipality offering emergency care has the duty to provide it, within its abilities. Clearly, a duty to act on the part of the town exists, and the town can be liable if it wrongfully refuses to respond without justifiable cause. As the paramedic is only an employee, and under no direct contractual relationship with the patient, he or she may escape liability for refusing or failing to respond.

Even where a contractual relationship does exist, failure to respond may be excused for a good cause, including:

- a common disaster that exhausts EMS capabilities.
- determining that the patient requires services that are beyond the scope of the contract, or the capabilities, of EMS to provide.
- a "good faith" belief that emergency care is not required.

- prior breach of agreement (i.e., "nonpayment") by the patient or municipality, where adequate notice of the breach and termination of services is provided.

2.   When You Begin To Act

Starting treatment automatically imposes the duty on you to see the treatment through to its conclusion, even though you had no duty to act in the first place. Simply stated, once you start treatment you cannot stop.

This is a difficult proposition for most people to understand. They ask, if they had no obligation to begin aid, why can't they stop or lessen their involvement whenever they choose? The legal reasoning is based on the possibility that the patient may have refused aid from others and is relying on your continued assistance.

What constitutes "commencement" of treatment to require continued treatment is also a question of fact that must be determined.

If an EMT without a contractual duty to act stops and merely inquires about the condition of motorists injured in an accident, in my opinion that would not be commencement of the treatment. I would reach an opposite conclusion if the EMT examined the motorists or took other action to assist them.

From a legal viewpoint, it is best not to begin treating a patient unless you plan to render all the aid required of you had the duty to otherwise existed.

1. Do not stop or become involved unnecessarily.

2. Clearly advise possible patients that you cannot render aid so your position is definite.

3. You can summons others to help because it does not constitute "commencement of treatment."

4. If you do start to render assistance, make certain that you stay with the patient, and provide all the aid possible until the patient is in the hands of other personnel with equal or greater competence.

Define beforehand who you must treat. Be cautious in deciding whether you will commence aid where no duty otherwise exists, and make certain to provide the best possible care to all patients you do treat.

3.   Duty Exists to Anyone Who May Be Injured Through Your Negligent Acts

Duty to act in a non-negligent manner extends not only to patients, but to others who may be injured through your negligence. This is the basis for imposing negligence in an auto accident—each driver has a duty to other motorists and pedestrians within a radius where they could be injured. An EMT negligently operating an ambulance has the duty of non-negligent vehicle use to all who could sustain injury.

Duty can take many forms. The only time where it can be called into question is when you fail to act. However, if a court determines you should have acted, but didn't, the legal consequences can be severe.

THE "STANDARD OF CARE" YOU OWE THE PATIENT

In most malpractice cases the issue of duty is easily established, particularly where the accusation is based on EMS personnel performing negligent rather than "no" treatment.

The central issue in negligence litigation commonly is that of whether the defendant breached the "standard of care" owed the plaintiff. In a typical case 80–90 percent of all evidence will involve this one issue and it is routinely the most contested aspect of a case.

Breach of the "standard of care" means that the defendant's conduct did not conform with the reasonable level of skill, prudence, caution, and competence that could be expected under the circumstances.

But when does treatment fall below that required standard? Often this is not easily decided as the entire process is very debatable and may involve "non-obvious" or highly technical errors.

If an EMT is a defendant, the question may be posed as "would other EMTs have performed in the same way?" Essentially the "standard" is determined by having the court conclude through evidence what others with equal training or certification would have done under the same circumstances. Through this process a "peer" standard is determined, and then the conduct of the defendant is evaluated to see whether he or she operated within the standard or below it. Even this approach requires further steps. For example, what standards will be operative?

A First Responder is expected to act as a reasonably prudent First Responder. An EMT with only basic life support training could not be expected to show the same skill as a paramedic with advanced life support training. What is expected of an emergency care physician would understandably be above that demanded from other EMS personnel without medical licensure. This is an important point to understand. You will be expected to act as competently as your peers—and this standard will vary within the different groups of EMS personnel.

Even then it may be difficult to define the "standard" your performance will be measured against. EMTs know they will be compared to other EMTs—but are there different standards even amongst EMTs working in different geographic locations? This is called the "locality" rule. Some states take the view that accepted practice in one area may differ in another. To that extent they limit comparisons to EMT practice in the given area.

Most states have abandoned the "locality" rule and freely accept testimony or evidence from comparable EMS personnel from anywhere in the country. Consistent with this practice they look to a "national" standard.

Negligence claims can be categorized as either "malfeasance" or "non-feasance." Malfeasance is where the defendant performed an affirmative act but violated the standard. Non-feasance is failure to act where required, the distinction is of no practical importance because in either event the defendant allegedly did not conform to the standard of care.

How does a court determine the standard of care and measure compliance with it? Let's take a look at a typical malpractice case to find the answer. Assume that a patient suffering from a cervical fracture sues an EMT for negligence, claiming the EMT caused further injury by not using a backboard and immobilization technique.

The plaintiff will attempt to show that the EMT should have suspected the possibility of cervical fracture and, that based on that availability of a backboard, would be the prudent treatment. Of course, either the failure to detect possible cervical fracture, or the failure to use a backboard if suspected, would be sufficient enough to establish negligence.

The defendant may argue that he conducted all reasonable examinations of the patient and found no symptoms consistent with cervical fracture. In other words, most other EMTs would not have detected the cervical fracture and therefore would have rendered the same treatment.

The issue is, "would other EMTs have suspected cervical fracture?" The plaintiff would perhaps try to show that other EMTs would have conducted a more intensive examination, or reached a different conclusion given the same examination. Again, the defendant's objectives would be just the opposite.

But how does the court determine which side is right? They do it through evidence from which it draws a conclusion as to who is correct.

The evidence may consist of:

- Testimony from other EMTs who would testify about how they would have conducted an examination under the same circumstances—and the conclusions they would draw about the patient possibly having a cervical fracture. The plaintiff's counsel would select witnesses who would logically testify that they would have conducted tests not done by the defendant, or reached a differing conclusion, while the defense would try to find EMTs to testify that they would have done the same procedures and reached the same diagnosis as the defendant.

- Texts, training manuals, and professional articles to show what an EMT should do in comparable cases can be introduced into evidence. This helps define the expected "standard" and gives the court guidance as to what should reasonably be expected from an EMT.

Presented with this evidence, the court will determine:

- What the acceptable standard of practice is in detecting cervical fractures by EMTs, and
- Whether the defendant conformed to those standards?

Due to the subjective process, it is often difficult to predict the outcome of a case. Negligence cases defy a certain conclusion. No two cases are precisely alike, and each has its own unique set of facts.

Reasonableness of conduct depends on the facts and circumstances of the case. What is "reasonable" in one instance may not be in another. People do not act in a vacuum, but in an environment open to a wide range of variable circumstances.

Return to the case of the EMT being sued for not detecting a cervical fracture. Perhaps the EMT observed movement and no deformity, but did not check for pain, tenderness, or impaired breathing. Most EMTs know that there can be various symptoms to detect cervical fracture, and that the defendant EMT did not perform all the usual tests. Would this, in itself, establish negligence?

If the patient was the only person under treatment perhaps you can conclude reasonable opportunity to conduct a thorough examination. Now let's switch the facts. Suppose the patient was one of many badly injured people and there was a lack of EMS personnel. Wouldn't his failure to be as "thorough" be more reasonable?

Your liability does not increase because your judgment ultimately proved wrong. Physicians may recommend that a patient drop the idea of surgery only to have a disease later spread and cause the patient to die. Even attorneys guess wrong 50 percent of the time because every case has a winner and a loser. You are no different. Your liability will only increase when you fail to apply to the situation the skill and competence that your colleagues would employ.

Everything you do, or choose not to do, can be a source of liability. Although the possibilities are endless, we will discuss some of the common pitfalls encountered by EMS personnel in the following chapter.

There are two situations where your negligence may be sufficiently obvious to avoid the need for extraneous evidence to prove you violated the standard of care. They do arise in EMS cases and therefore require comment.

1.   Res Ipsa Loquitor

This Latin term literally means "it speaks for itself." Where an injury could only occur in the presence of negligence, and the circumstances were within the total control of the defendant, free of interference by the plaintiff—then the obvious conclusion is that the defendant must have been negligent.

For *res ipsa loquitor* to exist, common knowledge that the injury could only come about through negligence is required.

- An EMT accidently "backing" his ambulance over a patient does not require testimony from other EMTs because they generally do not run down their patients. This is common sense, therefore, *res ipsa loquitor*.

- What about an EMT who improperly "splints" a patient? Would this be *res ipsa loquitor*? Probably not, because the proper application of a splint is not a matter of common sense or common knowledge to most people. This could only be decided through professional testimony or technical discussions.

Res ipsa loquitor does not change the law of negligence, it only shifts the burden from the plaintiff to the defendant. Once the plaintiff shows sufficient facts to satisfy the court that through "common knowledge" he or she could not have suffered the injury except through the negligence of the defendant, he or she can rest the case. It is then for the defendant to show, if he can, that he was not negligent.

2.   Violation of Law

There are statutes, regulations, and licensing laws that prescribe what must, and must not, be done in the field of patient care. A law designed to prevent injury to a patient will be evidence of negligence, if violation of the law causes the anticipated injury.

- If state law requires a specified apparatus to be on ambulances, there would be liability if failure to have the equipment on the ambulance caused further injury to the patient.

- Administration of drugs by unlicensed personnel causing drug-induced injury is another example. The law was obviously intended to protect patients from the negligent administration of medication by non-qualified personnel. The violation created the injury the law was designed to protect against.

For a patient to win in a case involving violation of law, all he or she has to prove is:

1. The existence of the law and its intent.

2. The defendant violated the law.

3. The violation caused, or allowed for, the patient's injury.

Aside from the probable sanctions imposed by licensing agencies, or even criminal proceedings, EMS personnel should carefully comply with all applicable laws. To do otherwise can create a successful malpractice case for the patient.

PROVING THAT THE NEGLIGENT ACT CAUSED THE INJURY

This is the third element in a negligence claim. Not only must the patient prove that a negligent act occurred, and that the patient suffered injury or damage, but the patient must further prove that it was the negligent act that caused the injury.

In many negligence cases the relationship between a negligent act and a plaintiff's injury is obvious. If an EMT negligently operates his ambulance and strikes a motorist's vehicle in the rear resulting in immediate "whiplash" and other injury, there can be little question that it was the accident that caused the injuries.

The relationship between the act and the injury in a malpractice suit may be somewhat more subtle and difficult to prove, however. For example, the patient has an illness or injury that existed prior to the negligent act. To what degree did the prior illness or injury contribute to, if not totally cause, the harm resulting in the malpractice suit?

Let's see how this would work in practice:

- A patient's estate may sue an EMT for negligently causing the death of the patient by failing to, or negligently, using CPR. Assume further that the EMT was negligent. The question then becomes, was it the EMT's negligence that caused the death, or would the patient have died even with proper CPR? Clearly, if the patient's death was imminent in any event, the EMT cannot be held liable for the death as it was not the EMT's negligence, but unavoidable circumstances that caused it.

- Extend the argument on the above case. What if evidence proved that proper CPR may have sustained the patient's life for even a few additional moments, or that the chance for survival may have been 20 percent greater with CPR? Would the EMT then be liable? A court could grant a small award in the first instance as the negligence was the original factor in shortening life expectancy. Where a negligent act may even remotely be the cause of injury, a court can find liability. A plaintiff does not have to conclusively prove that the negligence caused the injury, as even a "reasonable likelihood" may be sufficient.

- Consider the case of a First Responder defending a claim that he was negligent in removing a spike accidently lodged in a patient's abdominal area. If the patient should go into cardiac arrest several months later, would the First Responder be liable for damages sustained as a result of the cardiac arrest? That would depend on whether the patient could reasonably prove that the cardiac arrest was in some way caused by the premature or negligent removal of the spike.

Consider, however, the difficulties the patient faces.

- Perhaps the cardiac arrest was totally independent of both the spike puncture or its negligent removal.

- Possibly the puncture rather than the spike removal caused the cardiac arrest.

- It may be that the cardiac arrest was brought on by drugs or therapy required to treat the puncture.

As you can see, proving the relationship between a negligent act and injury may require extensive medical testimony. Physicians or other expert witnesses used by the plaintiff will attempt to medically prove, or at least try to prove, the role of the negligent act in causing the damage. Defense counsel will attempt to show that no reasonable relationship exists between the two. It usually ends up a battle between experts presenting conflicting views.

One interesting question still remains. At what point is the relationship between the negligent act and the injury so remote as to be insufficient for proving "causation?"

Return to the puncture wound case. What if physicians administered penicillin as a preventive measure against systemic infection caused by the early removal of the spike—and the patient suffered allergic shock to the penicillin? Would the EMT be liable for the damages caused by the shock?

Of course, the patient can show a link between the negligent act and the shock. If the EMT had not been negligent by removing the spike, the patient may not have needed penicillin. Therefore, it was the negligence that created the need for the penicillin and brought on the shock as a result.

Virtually any following injury can be traced backwards. What if the patient was injured in a second accident while obtaining penicillin from a nearby pharmacy; shouldn't the EMT then be liable for those injuries also since it was his original act of negligence that set the chain of events in motion?

You may believe the obvious answer to be in the negative. However, the issue of "causation" is not confined to either a closeness in time or distance. In fact, the later damage complained of may occur years later, at a distant location and in a completely unexpected way.

The test is, what further injury or damage should the defendant reasonably have foreseen at the time of the negligent act? This does not imply the need for looking into the future, but only the ability to look ahead and consider all the potential results of the negligent act.

HOW DAMAGES ARE DETERMINED

A patient is not entitled to monetary damages simply because an EMS provider committed a negligent act. The patient must prove that as a result of it he or she suffered damages that are compensable.

Under our system of law, a defendant is not ordered to pay money because he or she performed a negligent act. Instead, it is viewed as a way of reimbursing the patient for an actual loss. In the modern malpractice case, the monetary damages can be large and verdicts of 1,000,000 dollars or more are no longer rare. Total damages due to a patient are a mixture of individual items that can be repaid.

The damages may include:

1.   Medical Expenses

The defendant may be ordered to pay all of the medical costs necessary to treat the injury. This includes hospitalization, physicians, X-rays, lab tests, drugs, and therapy. Future medical costs going beyond the date of the suit, or even within the life expectancy of the plaintiff, can be included. Medical costs paid by third parties (Blue Cross or Medicaid) can be repaid, although the patient would be required to repay the third party payor.

2.   Lost Earnings

The patient may have been out of work for a considerable period of time. Any difference between what the patient did earn, and what he or she would have earned, would be the liability of the defendant.

Often the patient cannot return to work or suffers a disability that prevents the patient from working at an original occupation. In these instances, the court would consider the patient's future earning potential in the past occupation, and the projected earning potential considering a new or limited work role. Future disability is never a certainty; however, the court must, based on medical testimony, determine whether a handicap to work will exist, and for how long.

3.   Conscious Pain and Suffering

Included in this category would be not only payment for pain and discomfort in the literal sense, but the value to be placed on the disability or impairment suffered by the patient.

Unlike other categories of damage, conscious pain and suffering follows a physical, perhaps even emotional, test. Accordingly, of all the damages, this one category commonly brings the highest award.

Look at it through the eyes of a jury. What is a lifetime as a parapalegic worth? What value do you put on the loss of eyesight? What would you be willing to accept for loss of function in your right hand? What is the "right" price tag for permanent facial disfigurement on a young female patient? Each of these injuries carries with it a functional incapacity, emotional or social impediment, or both.

Even a patient requiring hospitalization for several weeks, who will eventually be well again, is entitled to payment for the discomfort and the inconvenience of having his or her normal lifestyle interrupted.

To recover damages for conscious pain and suffering, the patient must remain conscious for at least a momentary period of time. Sudden death without the patient ever gaining consciousness will usually prevent recovery for this type of damage. Consistent with this generally accepted principle, if an EMT negligently treats a comatose patient who dies without regaining consciousness, the EMT would be freed from paying for the pain and suffering the patient obviously could not be aware of.

4.   Wrongful Death

Every state has a statute prescribing the method for assessing damages where a defendant negligently causes the death of the plaintiff. Most statutes define both a minimum and maximum recovery for wrongful death. Massachusetts, for example, uses 5,000 dollars as the lower limit and 100,000 dollars as the highest possible award, although many other states go considerably higher. What verdict the court will return as an award for damages depends largely on the method ordered under their state law.

There are two main approaches. Some states use what's called the "culpability" rule. Under this procedure, the court will set the award (within statutory limits) based entirely on the degree of negligence. Any degree of negligence, including slight negligence, may be enough to create liability against EMS providers. If a defendant caused wrongful death, even by exercising slight negligence, the jury would establish a corresponding award; while gross negligence or wanton, willful, and reckless conduct would justify either a maximum award or one close to it.

Other states direct the court not to the degree of negligence, but to the deceased plaintiff. Essentially they have to put a "monetary" value on a life based on such factors as age, prior health, education, earning capacity, family status, and general social worth to the community.

Clearly, each method represents both a blend of logic and illogic. For years, lawmakers wrestled with the problem of compensating for loss of life. Admittedly, it is difficult to define a method that satisfies everyone's point of view.

5.   Loss of Consortium

In a few states, a spouse is entitled to damages resulting from negligently-induced injury or death to his or her spouse. This is based on the theory that a spouse enjoys a "property right" and expectancy of full companionship. Any injury that creates even a partial or temporary disability can give rise to this claim. Contrary to popular belief, loss of consortium does not limit itself to loss of sexual capacity on the part of the spouse.

6.   Punitive Damage

I stated earlier that a court makes an award to compensate the plaintiff, not to punish the defendant.

In some rare instances, however, a court can in addition to the usual damages, order the defendant to pay "punitive" damages. As the name implies, it is intended to be punishment for the wrong-doing, with the intent to discourage further wrong-doing.

Punitive damages are usually found in cases where the defendant was either "wanton and reckless" in his or her disregard for the safety of the plaintiff, or where the defendant intentionally violated a law in the commission of the negligent act.

EMS providers performing in "good faith" rarely have to worry about punitive damages, although this is admittedly small consolation considering the compensatory damages their negligent acts may demand.

NEGLIGENCE IN RETROSPECT

As you can see, a negligence claim is highly technical. Each case requires not only the application of accepted legal principles, but the determination of many subjective factors. This is why every case can only have a possible or probable outcome at best, until the court reaches its final verdict.

Mere knowledge of the theory of negligence has little practical importance unless you can take that learned understanding and develop a conscious or deliberate approach to emergency medical care.

Considering the countless possibilities for negligence to arise in emergency care situations, it would be impossible for this or any other book to provide either clear instructions to guide you in making "on the spot" decisions, or suggest with certainty whether you did act properly. Indeed, what is prudent and professional in one instance may well be negligence in another.

In the following chapter we will discuss some of the more common situations that can, and often do, create liability. In Chapter 12, you will see some practical safeguards that can reduce your liability.

Nevertheless, your best weapon against the malpractice suit is still the competence—training—and common sense that only you can bring to every case you face in your daily practice.

As one veteran EMT reports, "I treat every patient as if he or she were a close relative. Then I know I'm performing to the extent of my ability."

Adherence to this practical philosophy can not only provide for optimum patient care, but also provide the best defense of all against the malpractice case.

TEST YOUR KNOWLEDGE

1. What is meant by "negligence?"
2. Would every act of malpractice involve negligence? Explain.
3. What elements must a patient prove to win a negligence claim?
4. Under what circumstances are you under a duty to the patient and obligated to continue care?
5. What is meant by the "standard of care" owed the patient?
6. Would the "standard of care" be the same for all EMS personnel? Explain.
7. How would a court determine the "standard of care," and whether you did or did not conform to it?
8. What is the significance in violating a law that results in patient injury?

9. Does a patient have to prove that a negligent act caused the injury, or would performance of the negligent act, in itself, be sufficient?

10. How are damages determined in a negligence case?

4

HOW NEGLIGENCE ACTIONS ARISE

One authority on emergency care recently estimated that EMS personnel may be called upon to provide over 7,000 different life-sustaining procedures. Even if that estimate can be challenged, all EMS providers recognize that their work presents enough opportunities for liability.

It may be impossible to highlight every possibility of liability and such an effort would be of no practical importance as statistics prove that the vast majority of negligence cases arise from relatively few situations. This chapter will consider those situations and show you the common reasons for liability, and what steps you can take to avoid it.

FAILURE TO TAKE TIMELY ACTION

One of the frequent claims that patients make against EMS personnel is that there were unreasonable delays in providing treatment and transport, and in many instances the delay caused the patient further injury or even death.

Emergency care by its very name implies an obligation on the part of EMS personnel to respond—and to respond quickly. This is probably the main expectation of the patient, and one that emergency care patients are quite sensitive to. Every moment a critically ill or injured patient waits for aid represents an eternity. When that response time is extended beyond what the patient (or the patient's relatives) see as reasonable, they can easily believe that the delay caused further avoidable problems.

When is a response time unreasonable to the point where it can cause liability? That will depend on many factors. The area of coverage may be the principle consideration. In metropolitan areas a normal response time may be 3–5 minutes, while rural areas may require 15–30 minutes. Undoubtedly, there are remote parts of the country where emergency care cannot reasonably be expected in less than an hour.

Another indicator of "reasonable response time" may be the written representations of the ambulance service itself. Many municipalities specify in their bid proposals the average or approximate response time to patients within the municipality. If a contract calls for attempts to achieve a response time of 3–5 minutes, it may be a sign of negligence if the ambulance did not arrive in 20–30 minutes.

Certainly the nature of the call will dictate the reasonableness of response time. A delay in transporting a patient between hospitals would not be critical; however, speed would be essential to a patient with cardiac arrest.

Generally, EMS personnel will not be liable for delay for reasons beyond their immediate control. Traffic conditions, weather, accidents enroute to the scene, and even unexpected mechanical problems with an ambulance or rescue vehicle can be justifiable reasons for late arrival.

There are definite steps that can be taken to insure timely response, or at least to avoid liability if service may be delayed. The checklist for timely response includes:

1. Do not contract for services that you are not equipped to handle. Proper service to a municipality may require 4–6 ambulances and adequate around-the-clock staff. Understaffing or insufficient equipment to handle the possible case load will certainly create a delay, and this delay could be negligent.

2. Do not bid a contract requiring a response time unless you have every reason to believe you can achieve it. One ambulance service represented under a city contract stated that it would achieve an average response time of 5 minutes; however, their trip reports disclosed an average response time of 12–15 minutes. This inconsistency can be evidence of negligent staffing and planning requiring additional staff and equipment to comply with the contract.

3. Do not indicate a response time on a call unless it can be accomplished. Some dispatchers will try to calm the concerns of a caller by saying "we'll be there in 2–3 minutes," and arrive 25 minutes later. The 25 minutes may be reasonable under the circumstances, but it may not appear reasonable to the patient.

4. Do not accept the call unless you can provide timely service. The proper procedure is to refer the call to an alternate service or other responder; or if alternate responders are not available, let the patient know there may be a delay—and why.

5. Make certain that your trip reports indicate the time of the call and time of arrival. A patient may claim that an ambulance arrived later than the actual time of arrival.

6. Anticipate reasons for delay. Adequate staffing and reserve crews

are a must. Predictable equipment failure can be a source of liability if delay was caused by improperly maintained vehicles.

7. Do a careful analysis of your response time. How does it compare to other ambulance services in your area? Your goal must be to reduce response time not only to prevailing standards, but to the most efficient service your ambulance or rescue unit can provide.

SCREENING PROBLEMS

Telephone screening of emergency calls is a highly hazardous activity. Every dispatcher spends time making a series of "judgment calls" trying to decide who does, and does not, require emergency care. Unfortunately, a dispatcher may decide a call does not represent an emergency, only to later discover that the patient died or suffered serious consequences due to the refusal to send aid.

Dispatchers and their employees can be responsible for liability if the screening was performed in a negligent manner. Perhaps the one central problem with adopting a screening technique is that there is little agreement on how screening is accomplished. Screening tends to mean different things to different EMS units, and the industry has yet to define a standardized system that works better than others.

The obvious difficulty with screening is that a "roll on every call" policy would put a strain, economically and logistically, on any emergency care system. On the other hand, a policy of very rigid screening would deprive some patients of needed care that could not be properly evaluated through a telephone triage routine.

EMS units have experimented with a variety of approaches to put the problems in balance. Some communities have tried a "tiered" method where questionable calls were referred to rescue units instead of life support units. This plan was stopped after a rescue unit responded to a referred call from a patient in cardiac arrest.

Some EMS units have hired paramedics and even registered nurses as dispatchers. However, these plans failed when it was discovered that there was no real change in the number of "dry runs."

Screening may be more legally troublesome to municipally operated rescue units than privately owned ambulance services because municipalities would have a greater duty to act, and in the absence of a contractual obligation an ambulance service may not have any duty to respond, even if it is medically unjustified. Further, most ambulance services receive calls from fire, police, and other First Responders who perform a screening function for them.

How can an EMS unit improve its screening technique to reduce potential liability?

1. Use only experienced and qualified dispatchers. Dispatching requires a person who has the ability and training to properly "screen" calls. It is safest to use personnel with similar backgrounds to dispatchers from similar EMS units.

2. Dispatchers must make a satisfactory inquiry to determine the patient's condition. A complete screening procedure can uncover an emergency need that a hasty technique may overlook. Screening should always include asking about vital signs, prior history, the possibility of cardiac or internal injury, bleeding, and whether the patient may have a drug overdose. What questions will be appropriate depends on the nature of the illness or injury. This requires a careful, thorough, and prudent examination and an equally prudent determination of whether emergency care is required.

3. The statistics of an EMS unit can to some degree measure the effectiveness of the screening procedure. Similar EMS units in your area may respond to 1 out of 2.5 calls. How does this compare to yours? What percentage of calls turn out to be "dry runs," and how does this compare to industry-wide averages?

4. From a legal viewpoint it is better to send or refer the call to a rescue unit or basic life support unit rather than refuse a questionable call.

5. The best policy is to "roll with the call" unless you are convinced the patient does not require emergency care. Doubt should always go in favor of the patient.

ABANDONMENT

EMS personnel must remain with the patient until the patient is under the supervision of other EMS units of equal or greater competence, or refuses treatment and transport through a valid nonconsent response.

There are repeated instances of EMS personnel facing liability on the theory that they have abandoned a patient. An abandonment claim can occur at any level of care, and even a temporary failure to supervise or stay with the patient can create liability. Perhaps even more dangerous are cases where EMS personnel prematurely or unjustifiably terminate or leave the patient without continuing care.

In practice, abandonment can take many forms:

- An EMT may leave a patient in an Emergency Department before actual admittance or supervision of the patient by the ED staff.

- A rescue unit may wrongly decide that a patient does not need emergency treatment or transport and leave him at the scene of an accident.

- A paramedic with advanced life support training may transfer a patient requiring that level of care to an EMT unit not capable of providing the needed treatment.

- An EMT may, in a triage situation, leave one patient for an unreasonably long time period as he attends other patients.

As you can see, abandonment is only a form of negligence. The liability focuses on the fact that the EMS personnel did not provide the continuity of care that the patient required, and that the failure to provide continued treatment or supervision caused the patient further injury.

What steps can EMS personnel take to avoid a negligence suit based on abandonment? Practitioners and legal authorities alike suggest the following guidelines:

1. Once you start treatment, or accept the duty to provide the service, then remain with the patient until he or she is safely transferred to the care of other providers with equal or greater competence. A First Responder, for example, should remain with the patient until an EMT takes over. Similarly, an EMT's duties do not end until the patient is under the actual supervision of the ED. An EMS system requires a coordinated link between various levels or practitioners. Ending your duties before the patient is in the hands of those on the next level is one certain way to run into the abandonment problem.

2. Do not leave a patient who decides he or she may not require emergency care unless you have performed an adequate examination of the patient, and are convinced that he or she is correct. In many instances, a patient is the least qualified person to assess his or her own medical condition, and if the patient's judgment proves to be wrong you can be held liable.

3. Emergency Departments represent a special danger to EMTs. Frequently an EMT will leave the patient with an ED before knowing that the patient has been admitted, or had proper consultation or that information on the patient has been given to the ED physician. Never leave a patient in an ED until you have provided the staff with all the required information and are satisfied that the ED staff is attending to the needs of the patient.

4. When patients refuse treatment and transport, consider carefully whether the patient has the mental capacity to refuse consent—particularly when the patient requires immediate treatment. If the patient's non-consent proves later to be invalid you can be held liable for leaving the patient. This is possibly

the one reason why cases that are questionable on the issue of mental capacity should be decided in favor of treatment.

5. Police intervention is another problem area. Frequently, police will interrupt or interfere with treatment. This does not justify leaving the patient unless ordered to do so by the police. You have the obligation to remain with the patient until the patient is removed under police custody, and it is clear that you will not be given the opportunity to provide further treatment. Remember, delays in treatment caused by the police do not give you the right to leave a patient.

6. Rescue units involved in a triage or disaster situation should coordinate their work so that each patient receives the continuation of supervision and treatment warranted under the triage. There have been cases where coordination has been so poor that patients with lesser injuries have been totally abandoned and been deprived of needed transport.

7. Do not transfer a patient to EMS personnel that have a lesser capability to treat a patient than you have. A patient has the right to expect increased competency as he or she progresses through the EMS system. If a patient does not receive the quality of treatment that you could have provided, a claim of abandonment will exist.

8. Always ask yourself this one important question before you leave a patient: Is the patient in capable hands and did you do everything you could for him?

Of all the EMS personnel involved, abandonment claims are most likely to be lodged against First Responders. One reason for this is due to the poorly defined nature of the First Responder's role. Police, fire, and rescue units, as vital parts of the EMS system, usually understand the need to continue treatment until the arrival of an EMT or paramedic. However, a co-worker, truck driver, or other nonprofessional administering CPR may not appreciate this need, or may readily leave the patient to return to other duties. Although the Good Samaritan laws can protect against negligence claims declaring abandonment, First Responders should give the same priority to continuing treatment as EMS personnel who provide the service for pay.

INADEQUATE PATIENT CARE CAPABILITIES

Can a patient file a law suit if an ambulance service fails to provide the staff or equipment reasonably needed to treat the patient's condition? The answer is yes.

By providing emergency care services, an EMS unit implies that it has the corresponding capability to provide the personnel and equipment needed to properly respond to an emergency call. Consider this problem from the viewpoint of both personnel and equipment to see just how liability can arise.

Many ambulance services and rescue units respond by sending only the ambulance and driver but, surprisingly, no attendant. Typically, understaffing is the result of trying to reduce expenses coupled with the unrealistic idea that transport alone, without "on-going" treatment, is sufficient. Nothing could be further from the truth. EMS units have an obligation not only to provide transport and pre-transport treatment, but adequate treatment and supervision of the patient during transport as well.

The one-man ambulance service presents a medical, and at the same time, a legal risk. How can a patient be adequately supervised and treated if he or she is left unattended during transport? Should the patient experience or suffer further injury during transport that could have been monitored or treated with supervision, the patient would have an excellent case against the EMS unit.

This problem frequently stems from improper screening technique. A dispatcher may decide that a patient's injury does not require an attendant and send a one-man ambulance to, basically, provide only the transport function. If the dispatcher's assessment is correct there should be no legal effect. When the dispatcher underestimates the patient's needs, or where a patient experiences unexpected complications, understaffing poses a significant legal problem.

EMS units may attempt to defend a one-man responder unit on the basis of not being able to anticipate the emergency in advance. If the patient's original condition seemed to require only transport, why should the unit be held liable if the patient experiences unexpected or sudden complications enroute?

The defense of not anticipating an emergency in advance seldom works. Courts generally recognize that in an emergency care situation it is difficult to predict what can happen, and therefore the prudent rule is to be prepared for any medical event. Any lesser approach will appear unreasonable in most courts.

This does not mean that an EMS unit will necessarily comply with the standard of care owed the patient with even one attendant. Where there are two or more patients undergoing simultaneous transport, or even a single patient requiring the continued involvement of two or more attendants, that level of staffing would be required.

Some EMS units respond to a call with the minimum of staff requirements and adopt the position that if further personnel are needed after assessment of the situation, further staff assistance can be dispatched.

Fortunately, this is not a common procedure because it can create two problems. First, the EMS unit can be held liable for any delays in treatment or transport in the course of the arrival of what should have been dispatched originally. The second problem exists in the fact that the patient's needs during transport cannot always be determined through a pre-transport examination.

In most instances, the problem of understaffing applies to ambulance services involved in pre-hospital emergency care, although it can exist even in cases of inter-hospital transfers and transport. Ambulance services usually reason that inter-hospital transfers do not need more than basic transport because the patient would not be released for a transfer unless he or she was capable of enduring the transport. Clearly, a reciprocal obligation rests with the discharge hospital to make sure that the condition of the patient justifies transfer, or as an alternative, that the hospital either provides physician attendance or warns the ambulance service of the patient's anticipated needs during transport. The failure of the hospital to take these steps will not necessarily excuse liability on the part of the ambulance service because the ambulance service has the independent duty to handle any medical occurrence.

What about the liability of the EMT driver who transports an unattended patient? Can this driver be held liable for the understaffing problem? There are no reported cases on this issue; however, it's reasonably safe to conclude that the driver would not have liability if he or she had no control in deciding the staffing policy, and acted prudently in assigning his priorities between treatment and transport. However, this does impose unreasonable demands on an EMT driver who on one hand wants to achieve the fastest transport, and on the other, to administer temporary treatment to a patient in immediate need. From a liability point of view, it is perhaps the classic "no-win" situation.

A dispatcher or unit supervisor who has the responsibility to assign personnel to an emergency run could be liable if his judgment was challenged. Under today's standards for EMS response, such a policy of understaffing would be difficult or impossible to defend. This should be an adequate warning to supervisory personnel and ambulance services alike whose primary objective is to reduce costs at the cost of patient care.

Proper equipment is another source of potential liability. To a large extent the problem of inadequate equipment has been controlled by strict vehicle qualification and lists of equipment required by state regulations and Medicare in places where ambulance service is funded by Medicare.

It is beyond the scope of this book to restate these requirements as equipment needs and vehicle specifications change from state to state and depend on whether the patient was to receive basic life support or advanced life support treatment.

There are three common situations where lack of equipment can play a decisive part in a negligence claim.

1. When the ambulance service operates without legally required equipment. Lack of working equipment, violating a state regulation that is causing further patient injury, would be at first view evidence of negligence.

2. When the EMS unit does not carry the equipment that is normally available in other EMS units, the unit is operating in a negligent manner because it breaches the standard of care owed to the patient.

3. When the EMS unit responds to a call and it is expected that the patient may require equipment that the EMS unit cannot provide. This underscores the obligation to accept only calls that you are adequately staffed and equipped to handle.

Improper housekeeping and maintenance of equipment and supplies can create awkward legal problems. There have been many instances of paramedics failing to replace emergency drugs; EMTs not able to find airway tubes, and even a case of backboards being left at the ambulance facility. Similar cases involve ambulances that start runs with the EMT aware of a malfunction in the radio system and one illogical case of an ambulance running out of gas during an emergency transport.

These errors may appear to be insignificant, but from a patient's outlook all he or she has to prove is that (1) you should have had the equipment, (2) he or she needed it, and (3) your failure to provide it caused further harm.

Review your own policies:

1. Do you staff your ambulance(s) with sufficient personnel to provide adequate treatment during transport?

2. Do you provide personnel and equipment qualified to adequately treat patients?

3. Are your dispatchers or unit supervisors qualified to determine the level of care required?

4. Do your vehicles and equipment meet all the regulations applying to them?

5. Do you provide equipment and supplies similar to that of other EMS units providing the same level of emergency care?

6. Do you properly maintain your equipment and vehicles so that they run and start in excellent working order?

7. Do you have a "pre-run" checklist to make sure that all equipment and supplies are on hand?

8. Do you add new equipment to stay in touch with the improved technology available to emergency care providers?

If you answered "no" to any of the above, you may have discovered a potential source of liability.

VEHICULAR LIABILITY

An area of constant concern to EMS unit drivers is the possibility of an accident. Considering both the right and the duty to provide the fastest transport consistent with public safety, EMS units are frequently involved in vehicular accidents.

EMS unit drivers do have limited protection as every state exempts them from observing the standard "rules of the road." Contrary to common belief, however, the various state laws do not provide absolute protection from vehicular negligence. There are a number of situations where an EMS unit can become liable due to negligent or wrongful use of a rescue vehicle.

Unit drivers can be held liable for injury if they negligently operate their vehicles unsafely, even under emergency conditions. Certainly, the degree of caution and care is somewhat different than that imposed on regular motorists as what is expected from a unit driver must be balanced against his or her obligation to provide emergency transport. Therefore, it becomes a "balancing" test. Did the unit driver operate the vehicle in a reasonable manner under the circumstances is the important question.

For example, a unit driver would have the right to speed or go through red lights, or otherwise ignore other traffic regulations. But at what point would speed be so excessive under the circumstances to be unreasonable? This is a question of fact that would have to be decided by a court; however, the court would certainly consider the condition of the patient, general traffic conditions, road conditions, the population density of the area, and ultimately the odds of the accident occurring by considering all these factors.

Referring again to the balancing test, a speed of 70–80 mph may be justified on a cardiac arrest case under favorable road conditions and on a rural road. Few people would call this speed justified for transporting a patient with a bone fracture where traffic is heavy. A resulting accident would cause liability.

Another view still used by the courts requires the unit driver to maintain sufficient control over the vehicle to avoid possible collisions. This imposes the duty on the unit driver to make sure that he or she has sufficient roadway clearance and that other vehicles have adequate warning.

Police and accident investigators point to these common driving errors by EMS unit drivers:

- Excess speed under the circumstances.

- Approaching intersections without clearing traffic coming from the side directions.

- Needless tailgating of vehicles that cannot or will not pull over to the right lane.

- Over-aggressiveness in changing lanes.

- Failure to consider road and weather conditions.

The right to provide fast transport does not replace the obligation to do it in a common sense manner with respect for the safety of other motorists and pedestrians. The interests of both the patient, and the public, must be considered when you are behind the wheel.

What about cases when the unit vehicle is not being used in emergency transport? In some states the "rules of the road" exemption applies only when the vehicle is used under actual emergency calls, and in other states it extends, either through meaning or enforcement, to any patient transport.

The statutory provisions in your state can make a difference. If they extend only to true emergency transport, then running an ambulance with a red light and siren for a non-emergency transport can result in criminal or traffic violations, and create a substantially stronger case for an injured motorist or pedestrian. Even where the state allows for light and siren operation in non-emergency patient transport, a negligence case can still arise if the unit vehicle was operated in a manner not meeting with the needs of the patient.

Of all the accident cases, the least defensible is when the unit vehicle runs with the red light and siren on when it is not involved in patient transport. There have been many cases where unit drivers abused their road privileges by running with the light and siren when driving a unit vehicle to a garage for repairs, and in some instances where the vehicle was being used for personal use.

There is a similar problem when a unit vehicle uses the light and siren when returning from a call. Many EMTs try to justify it by reasoning that it improves the retrieval or "turnaround" time for the vehicle to be available for the next call. Operationally that may make sense, but it still creates a weak legal defense. This is particularly true when the statute does not exempt the unit vehicles from the rules of the road after transport of the patient is made.

Admittedly, fire, police, and municipal rescue squads may adopt this policy under the cover of governmental immunity; however, this does not necessarily give private ambulance services the same right. The safest policy would be for all unit drivers to operate according to the rules of the road when returning from a call.

There is an added danger when operating a unit vehicle in non-compliance with the statutory exemptions. Insurance companies may not be required to honor their policies where the statute is not o-beyed, and an accident results. This possibility should be reviewed by counsel for every ambulance service.

Injury to motorists and pedestrians is not the only concern. A patient sustaining injuries would have equal rights to sue. In a few cases the patient's claim was not that he or she received a new or independent injury, but rather that the injury was sustained through the avoidable delay in receiving needed treatment. Coverage for this type of claim may not be included in the standard vehicle insurance policy. Where a policy does not cover this contingency, extended coverage should be obtained unless it would fall within the range of the malpractice rather than the vehicle policy. Unit drivers involved in an accident must give first priority to arranging alternate transportation for the patient and wrongful delay can be cause for an independent claim.

A final word is directed to drivers of fire, police, and municipal rescue vehicles. In many instances they do not realize their liability. If they negligently operate their vehicle, they can personally face a considerable judgment because their employer may be able to raise the defense of governmental immunity and may not provide the insurance that would protect them. Their risks can be appreciably greater than that of EMTs who would have their employers and insurance to stand behind them.

Remember these key points:

1. Unit vehicles should be operated by experienced and qualified drivers who can properly handle the vehicle and know their responsibility.

2. Comply with the statutes that free you from the "rules of the road."

3. Operate your vehicle in a reasonable and prudent manner keeping both the patients and public safety in mind.

4. Avoid any needless risk or driving hazards. Defensive driving is a primary requirement.

5. Do not run a vehicle with lights and sirens going unless they are for a medical emergency. Unless you have, or are responding to a patient requiring immediate transport, you should consider yourself just another vehicle on the road with no special privileges.

SPINAL INJURY CASES

Let us turn our attention to specific cases where liability can occur due to improper patient treatment.

It is only appropriate that spinal injuries head this list because they represent the most serious potential for monetary liability of all malpractice cases. It is easy to understand this fact when you consider that negligent treatment of this type of injury can cause a patient a lifetime of paralysis. The likelihood of extensive damage is only one dimension of the problem. It is complicated by the fact that patients with cervical fractures can be difficult to detect, and even with adequate detection, an injury can easily undergo further trauma.

Patients have the right to expect that EMS personnel will detect a possible cervical injury—and take proper steps to prevent further injury. Where EMS personnel cannot be sure of a spinal injury problem, they have the additional duty to treat the patient on the assumption that it does exist. It is only when the patient clearly shows no symptoms or possibility of spinal injury that preventative treatment can be avoided.

A profile of past cases indicates that improper diagnosis or treatment of the spinal injury patient may occur in the following ways:

- Rescue squad personnel may attempt to remove a patient from the wreckage without assessing the possibility of head and neck injuries, or remove the patient too aggressively where such injuries are suspected.

- EMS personnel may not place the necessary importance on checking for the possibility of neck and head injuries as they focus on the more visible injuries.

- Patients do not receive enough immobilization treatment. In most of the reported cases, EMTs failed to adequately immobilize the patient with cervical collars, backboards, and other restraints considered standard in EMS care.

- New technology can bring about new potential for liability, particularly where EMS personnel have not been adequately trained to use newer equipment. There have been some recent advances in spinal injury technology; however, not all EMTs use this technology or know how to use it. Either situation can result in a lawsuit.

- A patient's actions can make you legally responsible. An intoxicated person or one who resists examination for trauma requires special handling. EMS personnel must assert themselves so the patient is properly examined and immobilized if required. Allowing a patient to define the degree of immobilization can create liability, as you—not the patient—has the duty to enforce necessary treatment.

- In some instances, EMTs have failed to advise the Emergency Department (ED) of suspected spinal injuries and the ED then failed to immediately recognize and treat the patient as a spinal injury case.

These are a few of the ways in which a spinal injury malpractice case can result. There are other situations that can equally create problems.

One frequently reported problem involves complaints by EMS personnel that they have correctly treated the patient and communicated the spinal injury possibility to the ED, only to find the ED staff taking improper action. For example, an ED nurse may request that an EMT remove immobilization equipment before the patient has been examined by an ED physician.

Compliance with a nurse's orders in such a situation would create liability for the EMT because he has the continuing duty to maintain reasonable care, even while the patient is under the supervision of the ED. The proper course of action is to refuse taking part in any request that does not conform to the treatment the EMT considers appropriate.

EMS personnel should follow this checklist in handling patients with possible spinal injury.

1. Carefully examine the patient for spinal injury before you start treatment or decide on a method for removal.

2. Document the record with information on what symptoms you did, or did not, observe. If you decide that a patient does not suffer from spinal injury, make sure that your record indicates how you reached that conclusion. You may need it at a later date.

3. Treat comatose or intoxicated patients with special care. They cannot communicate their symptoms, and if the circumstances of their injury suggest the possibility of spinal injury you should assume it exists.

4. Where you do suspect spinal injury, make certain the patient agrees to all immobilization procedures. It is your responsibility to control the situation.

5. Do not go "half-way" with immobilization procedures. You cannot define the extent of the injury so you should assume the worst. Provide the patient with the maximum support possible.

6. As new equipment and techniques become available, use them and make certain you can use them properly.

7. Communicate with the ED before they handle the patient. It is your responsibility to let the ED know that a possible spinal injury case is arriving. You should notify the ED in advance by radio and upon arrival. Supervise transfer from the ambulance to the ED and do not leave until you are satisfied that the patient is being properly handled as a spinal injury case.

It all comes down to one word—"caution." If you have wrongly treated a patient as a spinal injury case you would face no liability because the patient could only complain of the temporary restriction from immobilization. Failure to provide the needed care to a patient with this injury makes liability likely. Do not worry about overreacting. Assuming the worst and doing your best is the only way to approach the patient with head and neck injuries.

CPR PROBLEMS

CPR is frequently mentioned by EMS personnel as the one form of treatment that gives them the most concern of legal liability. Perhaps the greatest benefit this section can provide you is to assure you that the likelihood of a lawsuit arising from improper CPR is extremely remote.

Of all the common treatments, CPR cases have the least chance of litigation. There have been no reported cases against amateurs providing CPR, and very few against EMTs and paramedics.

Why is this so? Does it imply that CPR is always provided in the proper manner? Of course not. Even where the provider is trained and certified there is a possibility of improper administration.

Lack of litigation does not mean a corresponding lack of negligent administration. The reasons go deeper:

1. A patient requiring CPR is already pulseless and not breathing. CPR can only improve the patient's condition.

2. Improper CPR is difficult to prove. Unlike most other forms of treatment, there is no solid evidence or documentation that points to negligent administration.

3. Many states protect amateurs who provide CPR by freeing them from liability arising from ordinary negligence. Further, immunity may be provided by the Good Samaritan statutes.

This does not mean that EMS personnel cannot be held liable should they negligently administer CPR. You can be liable if it could be proven that the patient could have been saved through continuous, and proper, CPR and you failed to provide one or the other. Admittedly, this is difficult to prove, just as it is difficult to prove that the CPR was negligently administered.

Nevertheless, CPR can create liability under the following circumstances:

1. If you provide CPR to a patient not requiring it, you can be liable for resulting injuries. A patient who is only comatose or faint is an example. Check the vital signs to make certain CPR is indicated.

2. Stopping CPR is the major danger. Too many EMT personnel prematurely discontinue CPR after initial efforts fail. This is a medical and legal error as many patients do ultimately respond after prolonged administration. Stopping before death is pronounced by a physician can be seen as abandonment of the patient and place you in the awkward legal position of explaining how you determined the patient died.

   Equally questionable is the practice of some EDs who instruct EMTs to end CPR after the EMT radioed the vital signs. A physician providing this instruction on the basis of transmitted information can be liable and can create equal liability for an EMT or paramedic who follows this instruction. There is only one defensible approach. Continue administration of CPR until the patient is delivered to the ED.

3. In my opinion the greatest legal risks in the future will be through failure to adopt newer CPR equipment. There is a constant stream of new and better CPR aids, and EMS personnel who fail to use equipment that can do the job better and longer than manual administration can be held liable due to their failure to stay current with industry standards. Mechanical devices are one such example. Can an EMT justify ending manual CPR due to exhaustion when mechanical CPR devices are available on the market? EMS personnel have the duty not only to provide CPR but to do it through the most effective means.

PARAMEDIC PROBLEMS

Paramedics (or EMTs with advanced life training) have legal concerns that go beyond those of basic life support EMTs. Their advanced training and range of practice gives them increased responsibility in telemetry, communication, devices, defibrillation equipment use, airway and gastric intubation, and the use of life-sustaining drugs and IVs.

The rights, duties, and liabilities of the paramedic are defined by state law. Some states grant the paramedic a wide range of responsibilities without physician authorization, where others restrict the duties of the paramedic to what has been authorized by a physician through transmission. Many of these states, however, authorize paramedics to act on their own when communication fails or is not practical and the patient's life is threatened.

Total compliance with state laws governing mobile intensive care units (ICUs) is a must if a paramedic is to avoid liability. Violation can subject the paramedic to a negligence claim and criminal liability, including the charge of unlawful practice of medicine. Considering the variety of state mobile ICU laws it is difficult to generalize areas of concern, nevertheless specific problem areas do seem to be dominant.

One common problem involves communication between the ICU and ED. Many paramedics fail to communicate the patient's vital signs, such as the electrocardiogram, to the physician. In some instances the paramedic believes he or she is legally competent to diagnose this, and in other cases the paramedic may not see the information as necessary to communicate. Failure to communicate and transmit necessary information can create liability. A corresponding duty rests with the ED to request information but their failure to do so may not exempt the paramedic from liability.

The key to the mobile ICU function is to maintain close and constant contact with the hospital base station to the extent that the maximum amount of physician supervision and control be maintained considering the circumstances involved. Any lesser effort must be avoided.

Drug administration is perhaps the one routine that most commonly distinguishes the paramedic from other EMS personnel. It can cause legal difficulty. Where drugs are administered according to physician authorization the instructions must be closely followed. Should the paramedic have the statutory authority to administer drugs without physician authorization, a standard protocol conforming to acceptable standards should be drafted and followed. Overuse of drugs has resulted in more cases than instances of under-utilization, but each problem has its own hazards.

Can a paramedic refuse to carry out a physician's instructions if he or she believes the instructions to be negligently carried out or harmful to the patient? The answer is a highly qualified "yes." A paramedic cannot carry out unauthorized treatment in violation of statutory provisions. With greater immunity, however, he or she can refuse to undertake an action that he or she believes is negligent. Paramedics have their own sphere of responsibility to patients and where they know or should have known that a treatment would be injurious to the patient they can refuse to act.

This does not suggest that paramedics should "double guess" the physician, as the physician has the primary role and responsibility. Clearly, a paramedic who refuses or fails to carry out reasonable instructions can be liable. Therefore, the paramedic should only refuse the instructions if performing them would cause obvious or unquestionable harm to the patient.

One reason for this potential conflict is due to improper communication between the ICU and the hospital. The physician assumes one set of facts while the paramedic has different facts. Clarifying and reviewing the patient's condition when instructions appear to be in conflict can usually resolve the question of wrong instructions.

Some states mandate paramedic compliance through a balance of immunity when the paramedic follows a physician's instructions. The obvious purpose in this legislation is to prevent refusal of treatment by paramedics. Under these laws, a paramedic has a virtual obligation to act and will have an expanded liability should he or she fail to do so.

TEST YOUR KNOWLEDGE

1. What factors influence a sensible response time?
2. What steps can EMS personnel take to avoid liability for delayed response?
3. How can improper "screening" techniques result in liability?
4. Under what circumstances, if any, can EMS personnel end treatment of a patient?
5. How can inadequate staffing of ambulances create liability?
6. What factors would show whether an ambulance service was negligent in not providing required equipment?
7. Under what circumstances is it lawful to run with a red light and siren in your state?
8. Outline a proper policy when treating a patient with possible spinal injury.
9. Why do so few CPR cases result in malpractice litigation?
10. Why is it important to maintain CPR treatment for a patient until he or she reaches the hospital?
11. Does a paramedic have a responsibility to transmit patient information to the hospital? Under your state law, what treatment can a paramedic provide without physician authorization?

5
DEFENSES TO THE NEGLIGENCE CLAIM

Defendants in a negligence case generally defend the claim by challenging the plaintiff's accusation that a negligent act occurred. Typically, the defendant will attempt to show the court that one or more of the essential elements to the negligence claim—duty, violation, causation, or harm—does not exist. Those defenses, however, only go to the main points of the plaintiff's case. In addition, a defendant may be able to raise "affirmative" defenses that would bar recovery even if the plaintiff can prove his case. In this chapter we will review several of the more common affirmative defenses that are often available to emergency care personnel.

GOOD SAMARITAN LAWS

Every state has passed Good Samaritan laws to protect citizens from liability when providing emergency medical care. The concept is logically based on the premise that a person who voluntarily stops to aid another should not be liable if he or she negligently provides that aid. The best part of the Good Samaritan laws is to not only protect the person providing aid, but to encourage people to freely assist others in distress by granting them immunity. It requires little imagination to predict that few people would risk liability through voluntary involvement, without the protection of these laws.

The degree to which Good Samaritan laws shield emergency care providers depends on whether the providers or their actions fall within the protection of the statute of their state. Many EMS personnel mistakenly believe that they are automatically protected by the Good Samaritan laws. No such general conclusion exists. In all cases EMS personnel must carefully analyze their own state law to determine just what protection it may afford them.

There are notable differences in the range of the laws among different states. Consider these variables:

- Some state laws cover all persons rendering aid, while others limit the protection to defined health practitioners such as physicians and nurses. Where protection is given only to health personnel, it may also include trained First Responders and paramedics. Illinois includes persons trained in CPR who voluntarily provide CPR when needed. Untrained persons who attempt CPR are not covered by this statute. The Illinois statute underscores the importance of making sure what the specific conditions are under your state law.

- The location of the assistance may be narrowly defined within the statute. Some states restrict the coverage to "aid rendered at the roadside" while others give no geographic limits.

- In some states, the law extends only to automobile or vehicle accidents and others adopt broader coverage or give no conditions about the source of the injury or accident.

- Many states apply the Good Samaritan laws only to accidents, and others apply it to both accidents and illness. Even then there is disagreement because some laws include only accidents and/or illness that jeopardizes the life of the patient leaving well-intentioned Good Samaritans who render aid to those with non-mortal wounds unprotected.

What does all this mean to emergency care personnel? It simply means that the only way to determine whether you are protected, and under what circumstances, requires a careful look at your state law regarding your position and the cases you routinely handle.

Volunteer rescue personnel, including most First Responders, are generally given protection because they follow the legislative intent of protecting those who demonstrate a Good Samaritan reason rather than a monetary reason for providing aid. This would generally extend to police, fire, and emergency squad or paramedic units employed by the municipality, where the conditions of the statute includes such personnel.

At the other extreme, providers who engage in care for profit or expectation of payment usually do not qualify. This would include privately-owned ambulance services and their EMTs. There are several reasons for not covering "fee for service" personnel. Private corporations do not undertake the service for charitable reasons and, therefore, should be strictly accountable for their actions. Further, they can adequately protect themselves from liability by carrying malpractice insurance. Finally, private companies hold themselves out as having the necessary skills to provide the service they expect payment for.

State laws that are hard to understand can raise more questions than they answer. For example, the New Jersey statute is like that found in many states by giving protection to an "emergency squad." What is meant by that term? Who precisely can anticipate protection under that language? Would this cover an EMT employed by a private ambulance service who stops to give aid to an unconscious motorist while returning from another run? Would he be covered if his company was under a flat contract with a New Jersey municipality? Would it make a difference whether the municipality billed the patient rather than posted billing through the ambulance service? The problem is one of distinguishing the "volunteer" from the "fee for service" provider as this tends to be the objective in drafting the Good Samaritan laws.

Aside from the immediate problems of vagueness, Good Samaritan laws have another weakness. Although they protect covered individuals from "negligence," they generally do not protect individuals against the more extreme cases of negligence which are legally classified as "gross negligence" or "wanton, wilful, or reckless conduct."

A patient may escape the controls of the Good Samaritan laws by simply alleging gross negligence to take the case beyond the protection of the law. Of course, the patient would be required to prove that the wrongful act was something more than "ordinary negligence" to prevail; nevertheless the simple accusation may be enough to give the patient his or her day in court.

Even where the Good Samaritan laws clearly apply, a patient has the right to file a malpractice claim. Good Samaritan laws do not prevent the start of litigation, and upon the filing of a suit EMS personnel must defend themselves by raising the defense. The defense may be successfully used; however, the obligation is on the defendant to raise it when filing the answer (defense) to the claim. Should the defendant fail to raise the defense he or she will usually be barred from raising it at the time of trial or to get an earlier dismissal.

GOVERNMENTAL IMMUNITY

It is a little known but widely accepted legal principle that a governmental body cannot be held liable for the negligent acts of its employees. This principle is based on the theory that government belongs to all the people and to allow one plaintiff to sue and recover would jeopardize the property owned by the government for the common welfare of all.

Reducing the doctrine of "governmental immunity" to the daily concerns of EMS personnel, it would mean that if a First Responder employed by a municipality negligently treated a patient, the municipality could escape liability as the employer by raising "governmental immunity" as a decided defense.

This defense, however, does have its limitations. For a governmental body—whether it be a municipality, county, state, or even the Federal government—to successfully use this defense, the activity must directly relate to the business of "governing."

As with so many terms this too lends itself to differing conclusions as to what is the business or function of "governing."

In at least one state court decision, the court held that "providing emergency medical care is not a function of government and government can be liable for negligent acts in providing this service." Predictably, another jurisdiction reached just the opposite conclusion.

Factors to take into consideration when making future decisions may include whether the emergency care was in addition to a required municipal service, such as First Responders assigned to police or fire units, or is the emergency unit a self-contained unit. Where a municipality imposes a charge, special tax, or a use fee for emergency medical care, courts usually view the activity as private in nature and not a "governmental function."

Many municipalities bill for ambulance services provided by the city or town, and in these instances the likelihood of using this defense successfully is remote.

Interestingly, a governmental body can elect not to use their defense and let the body be sued. Essentially this makes the plaintiff ask the municipality if they agree to a lawsuit against them. Whether a governmental body will elect to be sued depends on such practical considerations as the nature of the claim, amount of the monetary award likely to be awarded, publicity and public opinion, and whether the municipality is insured. Both the Federal government and states have "tort claim laws" that define the procedure in requesting consent and in following up on the claim.

In recent years the scope of governmental immunity has narrowed. Courts are increasingly limiting the governmental functions that will be protected and in some instances immunity has been legally abandoned or judicially terminated.

Amidst this discussion is the question of the position of EMS personnel employed by a governmental body where immunity does exist? Unfortunately, governmental immunity does not extend to employees—only to the governmental body itself as the employer. The risk of liability on the part of the employee does not affect the "welfare of the citizens as a whole." Since the government represents that "welfare" the immunity will be limited to it. This presents serious implications for EMS personnel involved in a governmental immunity situation.

As you will see in Chapter Seven, a patient can sue both the employee and the employer where an employee is negligent within the scope of employment.

In most instances the employer will defend and satisfy the claim on behalf of both. Where a governmental body can avoid liability on its own behalf by raising the immunity defense, the employee unable to use the same defense will be forced to stand alone as the remaining defendant.

Unfortunately, many municipal employers tell their employees that the municipality carries malpractice insurance. This can create false security for the EMS personnel relying on this, for the insurance underwriters can raise the same defenses as its insured—the municipality, and the assets of the employee, would nevertheless be exposed.

I recommend that all EMS personnel employed by governmental bodies follow this procedure to protect themselves:

1. Obtain a legal opinion as to whether your municipality can successfully raise governmental immunity for the acts you perform.

2. If there is any question about the legal obligations of the municipality, you can only be protected by adequate insurance.

3. Insurance coverage provided by the municipality should require that the insurance company defend and compensate the employees. Coverage that only extends to the municipality is of no value to you.

4. If you cannot obtain proper insurance coverage through your employer, then you should take out your own policy.

Governmental immunity can be unjust to a patient who is negligently treated and cannot receive compensation. It can be equally unjust to the employee who must individually shoulder the responsibility of satisfying a claim. Immunity also presents hidden perils to all government-employed EMS personnel.

STATUTE OF LIMITATIONS

Every legal action (except certain capital crimes) must be started in a defined time period. This is referred to as the *statute of limitations.*

Various legal actions will have their own set time limitation for starting a suit as provided for under state laws. For example, contract claims commonly have a six-year period, Federal crimes require action within five years and anti-trust claims must begin within four years.

In most states the statute of limitations for negligence claims is between 2–4 years. However, the patient may raise other bases for a malpractice case, such as assault and battery, breach of contract, invasion of privacy, or other action, each having a somewhat different time requirement.

If a case is not started within the time allowed under the statute of limitations, the defendant can raise it as favorable defense and this would quickly dismiss the suit.

The time period stops once suit is filed. It does not matter how long it takes the case to reach trial providing it was filed in time. Assume that your state has a three-year statute of limitations. If a patient says you provided negligent treatment on July 1, 1982, the suit must be filed on or before July 1, 1985. A later filing would give you the right to raise this defense. Many states follow the rule that the time period is measured from the date of the negligent act to the date suit is commenced, as in the above example.

Other states, with increasing frequency, are now adopting the position that the statute of limitations does not begin to run until the patient either knew or reasonably should have known of the negligent act. This is often referred to as the "discovery" rule.

Its logic is based on the theory that a patient should not be barred from pursuing a claim that he or she did not even know existed until it was too late. Realistically, many patients do not know that negligent aid was administered until long after the date for treatment. In many instances the time between treatment and finding out about negligence can be several years.

It is not difficult to see how this can occur even in the field of emergency medical care. For example, an EMT may aggravate a cervical fracture causing further injury, although it may require lengthy examinations and investigations to pinpoint the error on the part of the EMT.

In most EMS cases, however, the date of negligence and discovery coincide due to the readily apparent nature of the negligent act or its effect. This is a departure from negligence cases involving physicians, pharmacists, nurses, and other health providers where negligence may take a more subtle form and show itself only at a later date.

For minors, the statute of limitations does not start until the minor reaches the age of maturity. The minor is given this protection because he or she does not have the means to sue until he or she reaches majority age; however, a parent or guardian can start suit on a minor's behalf during his or her minority years.

CONTRIBUTORY NEGLIGENCE

Negligence on the part of the patient can be a bar to recovery even if the EMS personnel was negligent. The concept of "contributory negligence" rests on the idea that a person should not be allowed to complain of someone else's negligence when he or she contributed either to the cause of the injury or negligently failed to take reasonable steps to diminish his or her physical loss.

The classic examples of contributory negligence defense are most often found in automobile accidents, where for example, two motorists negligently enter an intersection at the same time. If the court concludes the plaintiff demonstrated negligence, his claim will be dismissed if the defense was raised, even though the defendant was also negligent. The application of contributory negligence to EMS malpractice cases is not common, although it is equally valid where it does exist.

For you to raise the defense you would have to show that the patient was negligent to some extent as a participant in the treatment, or in preserving his or her condition once the negligent act occurred.

Obvious examples of contributing negligence may include:

- A patient with a possible cervical fracture who was warned of the risks but still insists that a backboard not be used. The negligent accusation against the EMS personnel may be his or her failure to properly warn of the danger or insist on the backboard use.

- An intoxicated patient who blindly walks into traffic, while the suit against an EMT was based on his or her failure to use necessary restraints.

In each of these two examples the defending EMS personnel may argue, what about the patient? Didn't his own negligence in some way contribute to the situation? This raises the question of when is a patient negligent? In declaring contributory negligence the defendant must state the same elements of a negligence claim against the plaintiff. However, the patient will only be held to the standard of care exercised by a reasonably prudent person.

The law does not expect amateurs to understand medical matters. A patient is not negligent because he or she fails to understand complex medical matters or their consequences. All that is in question is whether the patient acted in a manner consistent with that of the reasonably prudent patient.

As you can see, the patient will be held to an entirely different standard than an EMS provider. As an EMS provider you will be expected to have the competence of a trained professional, while the patient will be held to the prudence of the amateur.

Let's return to the example of the patient who refuses a backboard. Was he negligent? Such a finding would require the court to conclude that under all the circumstances the patient ignored an apparent danger that should have been foreseen by him. Even if you can conclude that the EMT was negligent in not providing strong warnings, the patient was told about the danger and should have taken adequate steps to protect, not disregard, his health.

The intoxicated patient poses another problem. What standard of care should he or she be held to in avoiding self-injury? Most cases suggest that due to a diminished mental capacity, it would be difficult to establish negligence, placing an even greater obligation on the EMT to protect the intoxicated person.

Patients will commonly ignore warnings, resist treatment, or respond negligently to their own situations. When EMS personnel take all required steps to treat and protect the patient, and the patient refuses treatment or proper guidance, the EMS personnel are free of liability and the defense of contributory negligence has no practical importance.

Some states use the doctrine of "strict contributory negligence." Any finding that the plaintiff was negligent to any degree will prevent any recovery. The majority of states now use the "comparative negligence rule." If the court finds both the plaintiff and defendant negligent, the award will be proportioned according to the degree of negligence. If a patient suffered damages justifying a $100,000 award but the court concludes he is 10 percent at fault, and the defendant 90 percent at fault, the recovery would be reduced to $90,000. Where a plaintiff's negligence exceeds the defendant's, no award will be allowed. From a practical viewpoint, patients may try to blame EMS personnel for their own negligent refusal to cooperate and act prudently in accepting aid.

When a patient places himself or herself in a position of further risk, you should:

1. Warn the patient of the dangers of his acts.

2. Be commanding. A gentle warning may not be enough to properly warn a patient. Do everything possible to convince a patient of the risk.

3. If the patient still ignores your advice, have the patient sign a release form telling the patient that you warned him or her of the risks.

4. Do not delay in giving your professional judgment to patients. You are the expert in emergency medical care, not the patient.

Contributory negligence and other agreeing defenses discussed in this chapter can be vital in avoiding liability even where an unfortunate act of malpractice does occur. EMS personnel should never relax their standards based on the probable availability of one or more of these defenses, as patients will be deprived the care they deserve and your professional reputation can suffer from a justified but unsuccessful lawsuit.

TEST YOUR KNOWLEDGE

1. Outline the Good Samaritan statute(s) in your state.

2. Do Good Samaritan statutes generally protect EMS personnel who provide service for a fee? Why?

3. What is meant by "governmental immunity?" Does governmental immunity protect municipally employed EMS personnel who commit a negligent act?

4. Why may it be particularly important for governmentally employed EMS personnel to obtain their own insurance coverage?

5. What is meant by the statute of limitations? What is the statute of limitations in your state for negligence, assault and battery, invasion of privacy, and breach of contract?

6. Under what circumstances can a patient sue for a negligent act committed under the statute of limitations?

7. How would you define "contributory negligence?" Would your state allow patients any recovery if they shared any responsibility toward negligent act(s)?

8. Is a patient expected to have the same skills for assessing his or her condition as EMS personnel?

6

LIABILITY FROM UNAUTHORIZED TREATMENT

One of the more serious problems constantly faced by the emergency care provider involves claims by patients that the provider wrongfully rendered treatment without the permission of the patient. Without proper consent a patient can start a suit for assault and battery.

Most amateurs think the term "assault and battery" means striking a person or causing this person bodily injury through physical means. Admittedly this is one common application of the term, but it can also apply to a health practitioner providing life-sustaining treatment to a patient if that patient does not agree to it. It is a well recognized principle of law that all persons have the right to decide whether to accept or reject treatment.

Within a medico-legal context, EMS personnel must take the necessary precautions to make sure that the patient accepts treatment and that the consent is valid. Of greater concern is the question of the procedures to be followed when consent is refused, even when the consent is necessary to preserve the health of the patient.

EMS personnel must follow specific guidelines to effectively handle the consent problems associated with intoxicated persons, minors, mentally handicapped patients, comatose individuals, and other patients who either refuse treatment or throw into question their ability to consent. This chapter will outline the proper, liability-reducing procedures.

WHEN CONSENT IS REQUIRED

A patient has the right to determine what shall be done to his or her body. Through countless cases the courts have thought this meant the right to consent to any moving or transport of the person, treatment, or any other form of aid or "touching" of the patient. It is not in itself a valid defense to say that aid offered to the patient was in the patient's best interests, or that it could be proven that failure to consent to the treatment would harm the patient.

To shift the decision on whether aid would or should be rendered from the patient to the EMS personnel gives the patient fewer rights in controlling his or her welfare. This is precisely what the courts say must not happen.

A patient may agree to certain activities and not to others. For example, a patient may agree to transport by an EMT yet decline medical assistance enroute. An injured person may consent to medical assistance and at the same time refuse transport.

Frequently a patient will readily agree to certain EMS assistance while refusing other forms of aid. In these situations the EMS personnel should confine their activities to the procedures agreed to by the patient. Later in this chapter we will discuss procedures that should be followed when permission is refused by a patient.

In a like manner a patient has the unqualified right to withdraw his consent and refuse further treatment. Continued treatment after the patient clearly withdraws his consent can equally be a source of liability.

HOW CONSENT IS GRANTED

A patient usually indicates his or her consent by voluntarily submitting to treatment. This is referred to as "implied consent." It is not necessary for the patient to really be asked whether he or she "consents" or to obtain a written or verbal approval. Consent automatically exists when the patient acts in such a way that a reasonable person would assume that the patient is in agreement with the services being rendered.

An EMT may advise a patient that "he is to be lifted on to a stretcher." A patient not reacting to lifting and transfer may be an indication of consent. A patient that voluntarily extends his arm for a bandage wrap clearly grants implied consent to the treatment that was to be given.

For there to be an implied consent it is necessary that the patient be aware of the treatment being offered. An EMT may advise a patient that his arm will be placed in a splint. Letting the arm be placed in a splint would be implied consent but would not be consent to a hypodermic injection. If the patient had enough opportunity to see the preparation of the syringe, and still offered his arm, then it could be successfully argued that the patient knew and understood the treatment he was about to receive.

Refusal (non-consent) may also be implied. It is not necessary for the patient to verbally refuse aid. Refusal can be assumed from the patient's actions. It may be a nod of the head, or withdrawal of a limb subject to treatment. The patient can show refusal by "waving" you away or a meek removal of your hand.

To a degree, measuring implied consent becomes a matter of knowing how to interpret body language. The question always remains, what would a reasonable person assume a patient wants based on his or her words and actions?

In some instances a fully conscious patient may act with total listlessness. The patient remains completely sluggish and shows no signs of approving or disapproving the assistance offered. Faced with this situation you should assume that the sluggish attitude means consent. On the other hand, when the patient clearly shows you that he or she does not consent, you should end your assistance. Many legal authorities say that non-consent should be positive. An uncertain response or no response should be seen as sufficient consent.

This is usually the safer route to follow. Failure to give needed aid, without a clear showing of non-consent, can result in a negligence claim. However, if the court believes that the patient did not grant consent, but the patient did receive timely and needed aid, then obviously you would have a more defendable position. This assumes that the patient is conscious and has no mental disability. Basically the theory is that a person who has the ability to refuse consent and takes no action supporting that refusal is assumed to have consented.

INFORMED CONSENT AND EMERGENCY MEDICAL CARE

The word "consent" alone means little. For the consent to be valid, the patient must have enough information and knowledge about what he or she is consenting to.

Applying the doctrine of informed consent to a medical setting is complex. Before a patient can provide the informed consent—which is the only valid consent—the patient must understand (1) the nature of the illness or injury, (2) the treatment recommended, (3) the possible or foreseeable risks and dangers that may result from the treatment, (4) alternative treatments possible—and their risks, and (5) the dangers of refusing treatment.

Since emergency medical care involves only immediate treatment for acute disorders, the concept of informed consent has a greatly reduced role. As treatment becomes more extensive, the need to "inform" becomes clearer. A physician in an ED is required to adequately advise a patient about a possible amputation; however, a First Responder is not required to explain the need for a tourniquet or splint.

As a First Responder or EMT you should tell patients what they should know about the treatment being offered. This information should be stated in language that the patient can understand. Not only will this satisfy the requirements of "informed consent," but it will usually provide patients with greater confidence as they will know what to expect.

You may be under a greater obligation to explain the consequences of refusing aid. When assistance is refused, you should explain again what you propose for treatment, why it is necessary, and what can happen if the treatment is refused. A patient can argue that you were negligent for not telling him or her the results of non-consent.

PROCEDURES TO FOLLOW WHEN A PATIENT REFUSES CONSENT

Every emergency care provider can remember situations where a fully conscious, mentally competent adult refused needed assistance. This may be one of the most challenging and perhaps frustrating encounters in your profession. It may be obvious to you that a patient requires aid and the lack of prompt assistance will seriously jeopardize the patient, yet for some unknown reason the patient consistently and emphatically refuses help.

There are countless reasons for this. Some of the more common reasons include:

1. The patient may be disoriented and as a natural "withdrawal" reaction to this disorientation, refuse treatment.

2. Movement or assistance may cause actual or anticipated pain or trauma to the injured part.

3. The patient may believe that assistance will cause permanent injury, particularly in cases of cervical or spinal fracture.

4. Some patients may simply have more confidence in delaying treatment until a physician can examine and treat him or her.

5. The patient may refuse treatment due to religious grounds.

6. In some cases the refusal may be due to the attitude or behavior of the emergency care personnel; however, in most instances the refusal is not based on personal considerations or relationships with the EMS personnel. Therefore, you should not consider refusal as a personal rejection or a challenge to your competency. The patient may have reasons of his or her own that may or may not be to effectively communicated to you.

Whatever the reason given for refusing medical care, or even if no reason is given, the patient can reject aid or transport provided he or she has the mental capacity to do so.

One exception to this rule is the case where a patient refuses to be moved, and relocating the patient is necessary to let traffic move or is otherwise necessary for the public good. For example, a patient injured in an automobile accident can be removed from the scene of the accident so that the car can be moved and traffic resumed. This is a situation commonly encountered by police, fire personnel, and other First Responders. One question remains, where should the patient be moved to?

Given the conflict between a patient's refusal to be moved and the need to move the patient for the "public good," the First Responder should relocate the patient to the nearest location that provides reasonable comfort and protection to the patient. This location may be the roadside or, preferably, a nearby home or other shelter. Excessive transport to a hospital, even though logical and medically indicated, may constitute an "unauthorized transport" of the patient.

In every situation where a patient refuses either transport or aid, or withdraws consent for further assistance, the following procedures should be followed:

1. Clearly advise the patient of his or her medical condition and what you propose to do, and why the assistance is necessary. Make certain the patient understands this. Ask the patient if he or she fully understands what you are saying because patients often refuse aid without fully understanding their medical conditions or the need for immediate treatment.

2. Once you are satisfied that the patient fully understands the situation, make certain that his or her refusal to grant consent is crystal-clear and absolute. If you believe the patient is just undecided or could change his or her mind, you should continue to encourage consent.

3. Obtaining consent from a reluctant patient is similar to "selling." You may be unsuccessful in your approach, but often another EMT, First Responder or even a co-worker, friend, or bystander at the scene of an accident may use an approach that will work. Encourage involvement by others at the scene.

4. Do not be hasty. Many patients will first refuse aid and after a short period of time change their mind. You should stay with the patient—and continue to ask for his or her consent until the patient is either in the hands of other emergency care personnel, or voluntarily leaves the scene of the accident.

5. Make certain you have witnesses. All too often a patient will refuse consent and then deny it, claiming that the EMS per-

sonnel were negligent in not giving the necessary aid. Do not let the situation become a matter of your word against theirs. The witnesses should observe your efforts to obtain consent and the refusal. You should record the names and addresses of all bystanders who have witnessed your efforts in case you should need their testimony later.

6. Decide whether the patient has enough mental capacity to refuse consent. Minors, as you will see later in this chapter, require additional procedures. If the patient's mental state is affected by drug or alcohol use, or is impaired by neurological damage, or even trauma, his or her competency to refuse treatment should be questioned. If you have a reasonable basis to suspect lack of mental capacity, you should follow the standard steps outlined for handling the "mentally incapacitated patient."

7. Obtain a written release from the patient. A standard "release" may take the following form:

RELEASE

I, the undersigned, have been advised that medical assistance on my behalf is necessary, and that refusal of said assistance and transport may result in death, or imperil my health. Nevertheless, I refuse to accept treatment or transport and assume all risks and consequences of my decision and release _____ _____from any liability arising from my refusal.

Witnessed by:

_____   _____
                                 Patient

                                 _____
                                 Address

                                 Date: _____

Most ambulance services and First Responders have their own release forms that may be worded differently; however, every release document should state that (a) the patient has been told of his or her condition, (b) the patient understands the risks of refusal, (c) the patient refuses assistance or transport (or whatever assistance was offered), (d) that the patient assumes all risks, and (e) the patient releases the EMS personnel from liability. The release should cover both the employee and the employer. For example, an EMT would provide in the release that both "John Jones and XYZ Ambulance Service, Inc." are released. The release should also be witnessed by a police officer or, preferably, by a friend or relative of the patient.

If the patient accepts some assistance (such as transport) but refuses medical aid or a specific treatment, a description of the treatment refused should be noted on the reverse side of the form and initialled by the patient. A release form may not be total protection because a patient can later claim that he or she did not have the mental capacity to refuse consent or sign the release form. However, it can give you a reasonable degree of protection, particularly if you and other eyewitnesses can show that the patient was capable of making the decision to refuse treatment.

8. Even by following the above procedures carefully, and you have a signed release in hand, the duties of the EMS personnel may not end. You want to avoid any accusation that you "abandoned" the patient even though the patient refuses your help. Before you leave the scene take reasonable steps to protect the patient by notifying a physician or relative and, if possible, remain at the scene until the patient is attended to by others.

Each refusal of consent situation presents new problems. Although you cannot force assistance on a mentally competent adult who rejects your aid, you must be certain that you made every reasonable effort to get the patient's consent and then acted prudently to keep the patient from further injury.

SPECIAL PROBLEMS IN "NON-CONSENT" CASES

In many situations a patient will accept treatment or transport, but try to modify the assistance being offered.

Consider these possibilities:

- A patient may demand transport to a hospital of his or her choosing, even though the hospital is further away than the hospital chosen by the EMT. If the injury is not a medical emergency, and there is no danger to the patient because of the time delay in reaching the hospital, the patient's wish should be granted unless there is a practical or legal problem in bringing the patient to the hospital of his or her choice.

  Where the time delay could cause harm to the patient, the patient must be warned of the danger in extended transport. If the patient still refuses transport to the nearest hospital, the EMT should still proceed to the nearest hospital if the urgency for care requires it.

- Patients receiving treatment may accept most of the assistance offered but resist other procedures. A patient in an auto accident may readily accept all treatment but refuse to be lifted. A patient may decline to the administration of drugs but choose other forms of treatment. The patient has the right to decline all or any part of the EMS procedure. Where the patient generally cooperates and still refuses an important part of the treatment, the EMS personnel should follow the same procedure for getting a general consent, and document the refusal if unsuccessful in getting consent.

CONSENT FROM THE MENTALLY INCAPACITATED PATIENT

Until now, the issue of consent dealt with the adult patient with clear and full mental competency to decide whether he or she will, or will not, accept treatment. Patients who suffer from a mental incapacity cannot consent to treatment and lack the ability to rationally decline or withhold consent. Therefore, to protect both the patient's rights and at the same time provide EMS personnel with reasonable safeguards in handling the mentally handicapped patient, generally accepted procedures have been drawn up through case decisions.

What must first be established is whether the patient does or does not have the capacity or ability to decide the consent issue for himself.

Mental incapacity can take may forms, including:

- unconsciousness or being in a comatose state.
- mental distortion through the use of drugs or alcohol.
- injury induced trauma or shock.
- temporary but severe stress or depression or possibly temporary psychosis or other chronic mental disorder.

Obviously, the comatose or extremely intoxicated or incoherent patient presents no difficulty in making the determination. It is difficult to decide when the patient shows borderline rationality. Essentially, the EMS personnel must make a quick determination on the mental state of the patient to decide whether a patient can determine consent or not.

If you are in this situation, you should make enough of an examination of the patient to make a reasonable determination. Observe the patient's conduct, engage the patient in conversation and find out whether drugs or alcohol have been used. Once you have made the determination that the patient lacks enough mental competency to make a consent decision, see if other EMS personnel or bystanders share your opinion. Note your observations in your records as you may have to justify your evaluation if your judgment is later challenged.

Once you have determined that mental capacity does not exist, then your course of action will depend on whether or not the patient requires immediate emergency treatment. This is the second determination you must make.

When does a situation demand immediate emergency treatment? Some courts have defined it as an "emergency requiring immediate actions for the preservation of the life or health of the patient under circumstances in which it is impossible or impractical to obtain the patient's consent or the consent of anyone authorized to assume such responsibility."

If the life or health of the patient will not be seriously or permanently impaired by delaying treatment or transport until proper consent can be obtained, it is a "nonemergency" situation. Both the severity of the disorder and its immediacy must be established for it to be an "immediate emergency treatment" case. The mere fact that the patient requires medical attention or that it would be beneficial or improve the patient's comfort is not enough. Even if the condition may become worse with immediate aid it would not qualify as an "immediate emergency treatment" case unless the condition could deteriorate to the point where life or the health of the patient would be jeopardized before consent from others could be obtained.

As with the issue of mental competency, the determination of whether a case requires "immediate emergency treatment" must follow a thorough and reasonably prudent test. Many cases defy a certain or simplistic conclusion.

1. Immediate Emergency Treatment Situations

When a patient is not mentally competent enough to express consent, and requires "immediate emergency treatment," you have the "implied consent" to carry out the assistance and transport reasonably required to preserve the condition of the patient until consent from either the patient, or others acting on the patient's behalf, can be obtained.

The law refers to this as the "emergency doctrine." The theory is based on the assumption that a patient facing a life-threatening condition would normally act in his or her own best interests by authorizing treatment to preserve his or her life or health. Since the patient cannot grant that consent, and no one on the patient's behalf can do it within the required time, it is assumed that the consent exists as a matter of law.

This doctrine makes obvious sense. It provides for the patient who cannot act on his or her own the opportunity to obtain the treatment he or she logically would have accepted if mentally competent, and this allows EMS personnel to act quickly and with immunity.

There are cases where a person is incapacitated and another person with the authority to act on the person's behalf is present. If a husband and wife are both involved in an automobile accident, and as a result the husband is comatose but the wife is conscious; then consent by the wife to treat the husband should be obtained. Should the wife refuse aid for the husband it would have the same force as non-consent by the husband. Therefore, it is important to remember that the "emergency doctrine" only applies where a relative with the authority to decide the issue of consent on behalf of the patient cannot be contacted in sufficient time.

2.   The "Non-Emergency" Situation

Where "immediate emergency treatment" is not required, the "emergency doctrine" will not apply and consent from a person authorized to act for the patient must be obtained before treatment or transport.

Who is authorized to consent to treatment for an incompetent patient will depend on state law. It is important for all EMS personnel to know the authority relationships under state law and attempt to obtain authorization from the closest relative.

The following order of priority exists in most states:

- A spouse
- Either parent
- Any adult child
- Any adult brother or sister
- Any adult aunt or uncle
- Any grandparent
- Any person who has the obvious responsibility or authority to grant consent.

If a patient has a spouse, but the spouse cannot be contacted, then efforts should be made to contact the next closest relative until one can be found to grant consent. Should a spouse, for example, refuse consent, then consent from the next closest kin would have no authority to consent, as the consent or non-consent of the spouse being the closer kin would have priority.

Occasionally there are conflicts between relatives sharing the same degree of kinship. A mother may grant consent but the father may refuse. Where a conflict exists between relatives sharing the same degree of kinship to the patient, most court decisions hold that the direction of the consenting relative will take priority.

Consent by another can take the same form as that from the patient. In most cases the consent will be done by telephone. Since the consenting relative may not be in a position to observe the patient's condition you should accurately explain the patient's condition, what treatment you propose, and why. Many EMS personnel follow the policy of having a police officer or other bystander confirm the consent by speaking to the relative. This is a recommended procedure. However, you should always document the conversation by noting it in the record.

CONSENT PROBLEMS WITH MINORS

EMS personnel must take special care in dealing with minors. As a matter of law, minors do not have the ability to consent or refuse consent. It does not matter how rational or intelligent the minor may be—the minor's inability to consent always exists.

What is a minor? This depends on state law. In most states a person reaches the age of majority at 18. A few states still use the age of 21. Some states have passed statutes giving "emancipated" or "mature minors" the same status as adults. An "emancipated minor" is generally one over a certain age (but not yet reaching the age of maturity) who either lives apart from his or her parents and supports himself, or is married. Due to the differences between state laws, it is important to review the laws of your particular state to determine the issue of "minority age."

The approach to be taken with a minor is the same as that with a mentally incapacitated adult.

If "immediate emergency treatment" is required and prompt consent by a relative cannot be obtained, then you can provide needed treatment and transport under the "emergency" doctrine. In the "non-emergency" situation, consent will be required from a relative. Ordinarily that relative will be a parent or one having custodial or guardianship rights over the child. The consent of either parent is sufficient.

With increasing frequency, the minor will have divorced or separated parents. In these situations the consent should be obtained from the parent having custody. Where one parent has physical custody, but both parents share joint legal custody, then either parent will have the authority to consent.

Many courts adopt a relaxed attitude on the question of authority to grant consent. For example, many courts will take the position that a non-custodial father has "colorable" authority to grant consent without any indication against consent by the custodial mother. Unfortunately, as the rights of parents in custodial cases keep shifting, the legal rights and authorities also remain unclear.

Younger children are commonly in the care of persons other than the parents. Children injured while in school or summer camp are frequent examples. Many schools and camps obtain prior permission from parents so that school personnel or camp counsellors are allowed to issue consent in place of, and in the absence of, the parent. Presented with such a "loco parentis" (in the place of the parent) authorization, EMS personnel should still make a reasonable effort to obtain consent from a parent. However, if parental communication cannot be obtained, it is reasonably safe to proceed with treatment based on the written authorization.

Fortunately it is not a common occurrence, but there are highly controversial cases where a child requires aid, but the parents refuse consent. Many of these cases involve the parent spreading their religious beliefs to cover the child. This presents a problem for EMS personnel because on one hand they have a child needing medical attention, and on the other they cannot obtain the consent.

As with all "non-consent" cases, you should advise the parent of the risks, obtain a signed release from the parent, and have other bystanders witness the situation.

Whether the EMS personnel have any further legal obligation has not been reported in any legal texts. It is likely that no further requirement exists; however, some legal authorities suggest it may be prudent to report the incident to either the police or an appropriate child welfare agency, as they may be in a position to start court proceedings to allow treatment over the parent's objections. This action should only be considered where the medical assistance for the child is necessary to maintain the child's life or health and would be inappropriate if the health of the child is not in serious jeopardy. Upon court action, treatment would usually be at the hospital level rather than one of emergency care; however, the EMS personnel may be a factor in starting that required care.

HANDLING THE INCOMPETENT PATIENT WHO REFUSES TREATMENT

Adults who are mentally unable to consent and minors who legally cannot consent may resist "immediate emergency treatment." In fact, most reported cases of "non-consent" arise from the mentally incompetent adult or minor situation.

You have learned that in either situation you have the "implied consent" to treat and transport the patient if it is a medical emergency—and if consent from another party cannot be quickly obtained. The "implied consent" doctrine is convenient when the patient is cooperative or listless. What about the situation where the patient actively resists help or attempts to leave the scene?

The prudent approach is to try to obtain the cooperation of the patient through conventional means. If the patient still resists, stronger patient management action should be used. It is much easier to abandon the patient; however, that is not only against the guidelines for proper patient care but it also can lead to a negligence claim.

Where you have the "implied consent" to treat a patient under the emergency doctrine, you can use any reasonable force to restrain the patient so that he or she does not cause further injury to himself or others. Many of these patients may have a serious mental disorder or suicidal tendencies. Others may suffer from drug overdose or hallucinogenic effects. Intoxicated persons demonstrate their own brand of irrationality and abuse. Minors may show a rebellious attitude, and all persons in this category may have more rational reasons to resist or run away—whether it be to escape from the scene of a crime or from incriminating evidence, or perhaps only because of a compromising or embarrassing situation. The purpose of restraint in each of these cases is not to arrest, but to protect the patient and others from his or her irrationality, and to subdue the patient to give the needed medical care.

The proper approach depends on the facts and circumstances of a given case. Prior court decisions encourage the concept that EMS personnel use all the force reasonably required to restrain the patient. What constitutes "reasonable force" depends on the degree of resistance on the part of the patient. Clearly, EMS personnel are not required to put themselves in danger of physical harm. If a patient uses excessive force to resist, you should delay giving aid until the police can handle the patient. Psychiatric patients may fall within this category; however, their treatment is discussed more in Chapter Eight.

WHY QUESTIONABLE CASES SHOULD BE DECIDED IN FAVOR OF TREATMENT

As you review this chapter you will find many situations where the question of whether you should render aid is in conflict with the question of consent.

Consider once again all the "on-the-spot" decisions you will have to make:

- Is the patient competent enough to give or refuse consent?
- Is the injury or illness severe enough to be a medical emergency?
- Is a person offering consent for a patient legally authorized?
- Do the patient's acts or words really constitute "non-consent?"
- Should you leave a resisting or abusive patient, or attempt to restrain and force treatment?

Whether you choose to treat a patient depends on your assessment of these points. More often than not you will have doubts about which path to follow. Faced with questionable consent problems, you should generally favor the decision to treat. If you are to be in error, it is considerably safer to err on the side of patient care. Not only is it in line with your professional duties and of benefit to the patient, but it is a much safer legal posture.

If you decide to treat, the patient may file a suit for assault and battery. But what are the patient's damages? How sympathetic will a jury be to a patient who complains that your "wrong" amounted to giving him the treatment needed for his own welfare? His claim at best is theoretical but seldom practical.

Now reverse the picture. Avoid treatment and the patient may claim that your refusal to render aid was legally unjustified. He may claim that he was incompetent to refuse while you thought he may have been competent. Perhaps he will argue that he did consent, or that he did require immediate emergency care where you thought otherwise. With those arguments he may state that your failure to act caused him serious harm which may not be too difficult to prove when needed aid is not provided.

Finally, the patient may convince a jury that you did not act safely. You will be shown as a professional who abandoned a patient. This is a difficult case to defend. This does not suggest that you should force treatment where consent clearly does not exist. I do suggest, however, that you act carefully and in favor of the patient's welfare where doubt exists. This is the one rule that can guide you through the cases that defy the clear answer.

TEST YOUR KNOWLEDGE

1. Why would treatment to a non-consenting patient with the ability to refuse help be considered assault and battery?
2. Can a mentally competent patient refuse treatment and transport if he or she needs immediate medical assistance?
3. When is consent "implied?"

4. Does a patient have the right to withdraw consent to treatment or transport once he or she agrees to it?

5. What is the "emergency doctrine?" Under what circumstances can it justify treatment without patient consent?

6. Explain the circumstances when you can provide treatment and transport to a patient who refuses aid.

7. Can you provide treatment or transport to a minor who consents if the minor is not in need of treatment to preserve life or health? Would your answer be different if the minor refused consent?

8. How would you decide whether a patient has the mental capacity to give consent?

9. What steps should you follow if:
   (a) An adult patient with mental capacity refuses assistance.
   (b) An intoxicated person refuses aid, but requires emergency treatment.
   (c) A 17-year-old patient requires assistance, but it is not necessarily an emergency.
   (d) An adult patient is found comatose.
   (e) An adult patient with mental capacity agrees to transport but refuses life-sustaining treatment during transport.
   (f) A child is seriously injured in school, the teacher consents to treatment, but neither parent can be located.
   (g) A brother and two sisters are involved in a car accident. The brother is comatose with suspected spinal injury. One sister consents to treatment and transport while the other is hysterical and strongly resists moving or treating the patient.

10. Why should questionable "consent" cases be decided in favor of treatment and transport.

11. Can you use reasonable force to restrain a patient who does not have the capacity to give or withhold consent, but is in need of emergency care? Would your answer be the same if he did not need emergency care? Explain.

7

LIABILITY FOR THE ACTS OF OTHERS

Malpractice cases in an emergency care situation seldom involve only one potential defendant. Even where the negligent act may be confined to one individual, the question is invariably asked, who else can be responsible?

Consider the possibilities. If an EMT is negligent, what is the amount of liability of his employer? Can a unit supervisor be liable for the negligent acts of a subordinate? What is the liability of an attending emergency care physician if a paramedic performs a wrongful act under the physician's supervision? How about the example of two or more EMS personnel jointly making an error in judgment?

Each of these questions underscores the importance of realizing that you may be liable for someone else's negligent performance—and they in turn may be responsible for yours. This chapter will discuss the various relationships in EMS to define these particular obligations.

LIABILITY OF AN EMPLOYER

The most frequent example of one party being responsible for the act of another is found in the employer-employee situation.

An employer is automatically liable for the acts of an employee performed within the scope of his or her duties. This is based on the universally accepted doctrine of *"Respondeat Superior"* ("let the master respond or answer for the acts of his employees"). This logic is found in the facts that:

1. The employer was in a position to control the employee.

2. The employee was working to further the interests of the employer.

3. As between an employer and a third party injured by a negligent employee, the risk of loss should fall upon the employer.

The doctrine of *"Respondeat Superior"* does not shift the liability from the employee to the employer because every person committing a wrong is liable for his or her own act. Rather, it gives the patient reason to act against both the employee *and* employer.

Let's put this into focus. Assume an EMT employed by an ambulance service negligently treats a patient causing 100,000 dollars in injuries. The patient can sue both the EMT (as the negligent party) and the ambulance service (as the employer) for the 100,000 dollars. Since the patient was only awarded 100,000 dollars in damages, he can only collect 100,000 dollars; however, he can recover all, or any part, of the 100,000 dollars from either party.

As a practical matter, in most cases the recovery is paid by the employer if for no better reason than the employer is usually in a better financial position to pay or is protected through malpractice insurance. However, both employee and employer would have to defend, and either or both can be held liable.

For an employer to be liable the employee must have committed the negligent act within the scope of his employment. What do we mean by "scope of employment?" This is a difficult term to accurately define; however, it includes all that could be reasonably expected in connection with his or her work, or that may benefit the employer.

No reasonable argument can be made that an EMT answering an emergency call is beyond the range of his or her duties because this is his or her duty. But what if the EMT used the ambulance to make an unauthorized trip? Would a truck driver trained as a First Responder create liability for his employer if he stopped to give aid to another motorist and was negligent?

There are no certain answers when an employee performs an act that is somewhat beyond the normal character of the position, although courts tend to broadly read "scope of employment" to bind an employer.

Where the issue of "scope of employment" is in dispute, employers and their insurance underwriters can be expected to fight liability. At the same time, counsel for the plaintiff will try to convince the court that the act was part of the job, realizing that recovery against the employer may be the only way to obtain payment.

Employers cannot deny liability for the negligent acts of their employees within the scope of that employment because such a position would go against public policy. However, an employee can issue a job description stating what is expected of an employee. The job description alone does not prevent a court from deciding that an activity beyond that needed necessarily releases the employer from liability, but it can be useful in shaping the court's view on what the employee's intended duties are.

Employer liability is also dependent on the existence of an employer-employee relationship. Negligence by an independent contractor performing a service under contract does not place liability on the hiring party. Therefore, a determination must be made on whether the negligent party was an employee or independent contractor. In most cases the distinction between employee and independent contractor is obvious. Still, there can be situations where the relationship is not clear and it becomes the main point in the litigation.

For example:

- Members of a "volunteer" or "auxiliary" fire or police unit that provides First Responder services.

- An EMT who is on "special call" by an ambulance service who is paid by the day.

In each of these examples the character of the relationship may be argued. To clear up the relationship, the courts usually consider the following points:

1. **Control.** Employees ordinarily work under the direction and supervision of their employers. Independent contractors are hired to perform a specific task free of this control.

2. **Withholding taxes.** Tax laws require an employer to withhold taxes, social security, and other payroll deductions. Independent contractors receive full contract payment without these deductions. It would be difficult for an ambulance service to withhold taxes and then claim the person was an independent contractor.

3. **Intent of the parties.** When confusion over a relationship exists, the parties can specify the nature of the relationship. Normally a contract will state that it is an independent contractor and not an employment relationship if that is the intent of the parties and it follows the facts.

All EMS units should review their affiliations with any person acting on their behalf to determine whether the individual may be regarded as an employee or independent contractor. Clarifying the relationship now can save the EMS unit from possible liability later.

LIABILITY FOR THE ACTS OF INDEPENDENT CONTRACTORS

An EMS unit or other party using an independent contractor to perform services does not have "automatic" liability for the negligent acts of the independent contractor. For example, a town may contract with an ambulance service to provide emergency care within the town. Negligence on the part of the ambulance service or any of its employees would not place liability on the town; however, the negligent acts of the employer would create liability for the ambulance service.

This situation does not mean that a patient cannot bring an action against a party using an independent contractor. The patient may be able to indicate negligence by a party in selecting the independent contractor.

For example, a municipality using an ambulance service may have made an inadequate investigation into the competency or capability of the ambulance firm. Assume that the ambulance service has a repeated history of violating regulations on required equipment. As a result of this, a patient suffers an injury because the required equipment is not available. In this instance the patient may argue that the town was negligent in its selection of the service.

Parties using independent contractors to provide emergency care services have the duty to adequately screen the competency of the contractor and they may be liable if they fail to do so. Before hiring the contractor, the hiring party should:

1. Carefully check the background of the contractor.

2. Investigate past violations of laws relating to emergency medical care and past malpractice suits.

3. Demand that the contractor be certified and professionally and legally qualified to perform its proposed function.

4. Provide in the contract that the contractor will comply with all applicable laws and regulations.

5. Make sure that the contractor has enough equipment and personnel to carry out the level of care required, and that the contractor handle the possible demand for emergency care.

A municipality or EMS unit has the responsibility to determine that those acting for it have been reasonably and prudently selected.

THE "BORROWED SERVANT" DOCTRINE

You are liable for the negligent actions of an employee from another party if that employee was acting under your supervision and control. This principle is commonly applied to surgeons in a hospital who have been held liable for the negligent performance of nurses or interns (both employees of the hospital), because the surgeon had control and supervised the nurses and interns during the surgical procedure.

The "Borrowed Servant" doctrine can also be applied to "emergency care." Consider:

- An emergency department physician may provide emergency services for the hospital on a contract (independent contractor) basis. Negligence on the part of a hospital employee working under the physician's supervision can create liability for the physician.

- A physician attending to a patient during ambulance transport may be liable for the negligent treatment of the EMT employed by the ambulance service.

- A paramedic with advanced life support training employed by a municipality may be responsible for the acts of EMTs or First Responders employed by others if the paramedic controls the EMS team and has control over them.

For the "Borrowed Servant" doctrine to apply, the defendant must take the employees of other employers under his or her control and have, or insist on, complete supervisory responsibility over them.

This principle is based on the theory that when a person has control over someone else's employees, he or she should be responsible for their acts. This person stands in the position of the employer even though no true employer-employee relationship exists. EMS providers who normally supervise the duties of others must protect the interests of patients by making sure that all participants under his or her control perform properly.

LIABILITY FOR THE ACTS OF SUBORDINATES

Unlike an employer, an EMS provider with supervisory responsibility over others in an EMS unit will not be liable for the acts of the subordinates unless the provider also was negligent. Cases trying to establish liability against supervisors require the patient prove the supervisor was negligent by allowing conditions to exist that resulted in the negligent act.

Plaintiffs have tried to show health care supervisors negligent in a variety of interesting ways, including:

1. Negligent hiring or screening of the employee.

2. Inadequate training by the supervisor.

3. Improper supervision by the supervisor over subordinates.

4. Failure to have enough staff or equipment required for the service.

5. Failure to take the necessary steps to correct or control the actions of a subordinate.

As you can see, the accusation can take many forms. In each instance, however, the patient is claiming that the supervisor violated the standard of care owed to the patient by negligently performing his or her supervisory role. It is not necessary for the supervisor to actually participate in the negligent act. The patient only has to prove that it was the supervisor's negligent act that set the chain of events in motion resulting in the injury.

Supervisors, EMS unit leaders, and administrators of emergency medical care services can protect themselves from accusations that they negligently performed their role if they take the necessary steps to:

1. Screen the qualifications and training of subordinates.

2. Provide their subordinates with proper training.

3. Make sure that subordinates remain competent through continual training, educational programs, and skill development courses.

4. Delegate responsibility to staff personnel qualified to carry out the assigned duties.

5. Make sure that there is enough staffing and equipment to perform possible needs.

6. Check the performance of subordinates to make sure they know their roles and can do them properly.

SHARING RESPONSIBILITY FOR NEGLIGENT TREATMENT

One characteristic of emergency care is the "team" effort. Unlike physicians and dentists who provide treatment with little or no involvement by others, EMS personnel cooperate with other members of the EMS team, and with police, fire personnel, and possibly amateur bystanders who may help at the scene of an accident.

This creates some obvious questions. For example, how can a patient determine who was negligent, or not negligent, when he or she may have passed through the hands of perhaps one or two First Responders, several EMTs or paramedics, and even the staff of the ED? How can he readily figure out when the responsibility for one level of provider ended and another's care began? How can he distinguish between the liability of two EMTs providing care at the same time? Of equal importance, how can liability be divided when two or more providers took part in the negligent act?

As a practical matter, patient's counsel will combine as defendants everyone who could possibly be involved in the negligent act. It is difficult to evaluate liability when the suit is started.

The case involves the accusation of combined negligence, for example, where two or three EMTs were negligent in providing treatment. The accusation may also charge continued negligence as shown when an EMT and ED physician both fail to detect and treat a disorder.

EMS personnel each have their own areas of responsibility. They can only be held liable when they fail to act properly within their area of competence. One ongoing problem, however, is the blurred dividing line between those areas of responsibility within the EMS system.

Put the problem in perspective:

- At what point does a First Responder's duties end and an EMT's begin? The same question must be asked about the transfer of responsibility between an EMT and ED staff.

- What is the liability of one First Responder who does not have CPR training, assisting another trained First Responder, with CPR training, who negligently provides CPR?

The possibilities of overlapping responsibility and joint commission of a negligent act are endless and certainly no book can convincingly state what liability can exist in each situation.

Most courts hold that when two or more providers are involved in a negligent act, each will have liability for all or any part of the damages claimed. Some states take the approach that if the liability can be reasonably divided, the liability for damages will be divided in the same manner. Using this method, a court may conclude that one provider caused 20 percent of the damage and another provider 80 percent and set the award based on these percentages.

It is quite common in malpractice cases for one provider to "point the finger" at another with the objective of shifting the blame. It then becomes a problem shared by both the plaintiff and defendants of trying to prove who did what at any point in time. Given the crisis atmosphere of emergency care, and the short time for treatment, this decision may be impossible, adding to it the chances of shared responsibility.

What can EMS personnel do to avoid being involved in malpractice claims resulting from the negligent acts of co-workers? There is no simple solution, but practical steps that can be helpful include:

1. Each EMS provider should thoroughly understand his or her role and what is expected from him or her as an EMS provider.

2. When a unit responds to an emergency situation, each member of the unit should have a carefully predefined primary area of

responsibility. This avoids unnecessary duplication or even worse—leaving out an important part of treatment.

3. A well coordinated effort by an EMS unit should allow for a "double check" by other members of the unit to the degree possible.

4. Do not command or allow others to perform treatment unless you know their capabilities.

5. Do not tolerate co-workers who constantly fail to measure up to standards. Either assist them in improving the quality of their performance, limit their activities to what they can handle, or avoid working with them.

6. Defend yourself if you believe another provider is administering a treatment wrong. If the other provider has the main responsibility he may be able to make the final decision but you will have at least used your knowledge in the situation. If you do have the final responsibility for the patient's treatment, listen to your co-workers and evaluate their opinions.

7. There should be a complete and coordinated report on information about the patient as he or she transferred from one level of care to the next. Insist on providing, and receiving, all the patient information required for an orderly flow of treatment.

8. Keep proper records and document the case carefully. Note what you have done and what services others provided. This can help you pinpoint liability at a future date.

9. Remember you may be held responsible for more than your own actions. Both you and the patient have the right to expect the best from the entire EMS team.

TEST YOUR KNOWLEDGE

1. What is meant by "Respondeat Superior?"

2. If an EMT negligently treats a patient, what is his or her liability and the liability of his or her employer?

3. Why is the difference between an employee and independent contractor of legal importance? How would you distinguish the two?

4. Under what circumstances can a party be liable for the negligent acts of an independent contractor acting for that party?

5. Explain the "borrowed servant" doctrine. Provide two examples of how it may exist in an emergency care situation.

6. Under what circumstances can a supervisor be liable for the

negligent acts of a subordinate? Would the supervisor have alternate or "automatic" liability, or would the patient have to show negligence on the part of the supervisor?

7. How would a court divide the damages if two or more EMS personnel share responsibility for negligent treatment?

8

HANDLING EMOTIONALLY DISTURBED PATIENTS

The agitated or emotionally disturbed patient is a challenging situation for the emergency care provider and involves many unique legal problems. Unlike the sane patient who accepts and cooperates in his or her care, or perhaps even rejects aid, the psychiatric emergency may run into patients who do not have the capacity to consent and usually resist with physical force. For the EMS provider, a variety of obvious questions appear, including what can be done to restrain the patient?

This chapter will deal with the legal problems in handling psychiatric cases. It is wise at this point to first define the term "psychiatric case" as it will be used in this chapter.

Classifying a patient as a psychiatric case within the bounds of this chapter takes on a somewhat different meaning from "insane" used in the medical or legal context. In many instances EMS personnel are called in to aid patients who demonstrate erratic, bizarre, or even abnormal behavior patterns. No conclusion should be drawn that these same patients necessarily have either long term mental problems or should be legally classified as insane. In fact, less than 10 percent of all "psychiatric" emergencies involve people later classified as medically or legally insane.

The emotionally disturbed patient may temporarily suffer from:

- Effects caused by an overdose of drugs or the ingestion of mind-altering hallucinogens or psychosis-causing controlled substances.

- Alcoholic beverages that bring the patient to the point of intoxication.

- Temporary "anxiety" attack.

- Depression and suicidal tendencies.

- Metabolic disease.

- Trauma from an accident or circumstances involving his or her personal life.

The causes will vary along with the type and degree of emotional disturbance. Some patients may appear very calm and be unable to respond either physically or verbally, while others may be totally incoherent and physically and verbally abusive. Considering the wide range of cases, no one "right" course of behavior can be advised because the facts of each case must determine the proper action.

DOCUMENTING THE PATIENT'S CONDITION

The most important step is to first document the patient's condition. Handling the emotionally disturbed patient lets procedures be used that are not permissible for the non-consenting patient who has full mental capacity.

At what point does a patient show enough abnormal behavior to justify being handled as an "emotionally" disturbed patient? This, of course, recognizes a basic judgment, and in many instances the issue cannot be easily decided.

Your liability will not rest on the questions of whether the patient was, or was not emotionally disturbed but on the logic of your decision.

Therefore, special care must be taken to accurately record all the observations that support your conclusion. Your record should adequately and faithfully state the general condition of the patient. How the patient was reacting; responses to simple questions; evidence of drug or alcohol ingestion; statements made by the patient; and the patient's behavior, must be observed and stated in enough detail to clearly show that the decision to consider the patient "emotionally disturbed" was warranted.

THE RIGHTS OF EMOTIONALLY DISTURBED PATIENTS

An emotionally disturbed patient cannot legally grant consent to treatment, and due to this same mental incapacity, refusal to grant this consent may have no legal significance.

A "psychiatric emergency" patient wrongfully treated or transported without consent can result in an action against the EMS personnel for:

1. *Assault*—scaring the patient with unauthorized handling and treatment.

2. *Battery*—unlawful touching and treatment of the patient.

3. *False imprisonment*—unlawful restraint of the patient or wrongfully confining the patient in an ambulance or psychiatric facility.

4. *Civil rights claims*—may be brought against emergency care personnel affiliated with governmental bodies.

Additional legal problems can exist in treating the psychiatric emergency. EMS personnel have to take special steps to protect themselves from charges of sexual abuse (commonly cited by female patients) or negligent treatment. It is the patient's erratic behavior that resulted in the care and it is that same erratic behavior that may have the patient challenging the care provided.

It is easier to explain the recommended procedures to be followed in "psychiatric emergency" cases by considering the various situations you will encounter.

THE "EMOTIONALLY DISTURBED" PATIENT WHO CONSENTS TO TREATMENT

When a patient consents to treatment and transport the legal problems are greatly reduced. Consent is usually given through quiet cooperation or the lack of active resistance.

If the patient requires immediate care, you should start treatment without delay. Protection of the patient should take priority over the need for getting consent from a person who can grant consent for the patient. This principle exists under the "Emergency Doctrine" discussed in Chapter Five.

When it is possible to get consent from a relative of the patient, reasonable efforts should be made to get that consent. This consent should be gotten even when the patient grants consent on his own. Involving a relative should be sought considering the inability of the emotionally disturbed patient to grant consent on his or her own behalf.

Consent should be thought of broadly. If you are in doubt it is much safer to decide in favor of treatment, particularly when the patient is extremely psychotic and does not actively resist treatment.

HOW TO HANDLE THE PATIENT WHO RESISTS TREATMENT

The emotionally disturbed patient will usually resist treatment. The patient may be physically abusive and threaten the safety of EMS personnel and bystanders alike.

The principle question is, can EMS personnel physically restrain a patient and treat that patient without consent? To answer the question one needs an analysis of the patient and the harm he or she is likely to cause himself or others if left untreated. A patient may show erratic behavior and need obvious psychiatric assistance, and at the same time show no reason for hurting himself or others. A patient sitting on a park bench may show no emotion and be unable to communicate due to a mental disorder. Assuming the patient does not consent to treatment, can treatment be forced upon the patient without approval? To avoid liability you would have to show a reasonable belief that the patient would harm himself or another party.

In addition, the chance for harm must be clear and imminent enough to justify emergency care. Under these circumstances the EMS personnel may guess at self-injury because the patient does not have enough ability to care for himself. This would be reasonable if the patient clearly lacked the ability to care for himself and self-danger was expected.

Every form of erratic behavior carries with it the belief that the abnormal behavior can result in possible self-injury or danger to others, even if the exact danger cannot be determined or predicted. However, the burden would be on the EMS personnel to show that "reasonable basis" for any further injury to the patient or others would be the logical end result of failure to treat at an earlier time.

The EMS personnel are not in a good position because they border between fulfilling the patient's need for treatment and the patient's rights to avoid intruding on his or her personal rights.

These cases, however, are in the minority. Most "psychiatric emergency" cases involve patients with aggressive disorders or those who show behavior that can easily be shown as harmful to the patient or others.

Under these circumstances, you may treat and transport the patient without consent. There are two legal theories to support this. The first is that the "Emergency Doctrine" is carried out on the basis that the patient would have consented to treatment if he or she had the mental capacity. The second exists under the "police powers" exercised to protect citizens from people who can cause them bodily harm.

A person with a suicidal nature certainly has a leaning towards self-injury. An intoxicated patient can easily be foreseen as injuring himself or others even if it's through a traffic injury. In these cases, EMS personnel can physically restrain the patient and give aid without consent, or even give aid with the patient resisting it.

AVOIDING UNREASONABLE FORCE

Faced with a combative patient who fights and actively resists treatment or transport, you can use whatever reasonable force is necessary to control the patient.

What determines "reasonable force" depends on what force was necessary to keep the patient from causing injury to himself or others while treatment and transport are performed. Another way of stating this is that the degree of force used by EMS personnel can only be equal to the degree of force used by the patient.

Reasonableness is determined by looking at all the circumstances involved. The aggressiveness of the patient is one factor, but the court can consider the age, sex, physical condition, and mental state of the patient. Drastic or unneeded force, beyond that required to calm the patient can result in liability.

Restraints should follow accepted EMS procedures. Normal restraining devices include straps, jackets, wristlets, anklets, restraining blankets, and other approved devices. The EMS objective should be to place whatever reasonable restraints required on the patient as quickly as possible, and with the least amount of discomfort to the patient—and with the least amount of force.

In recent years the typical physical restraints have been added to with sedatives and tranquilizing drugs. This is particularly true in cases where the patient is already under the care of an attending physician and may be undergoing transport between psychiatric facilities. Drug use must always rest with the attending physician and should never be used by an EMT without physician authorization.

Just as drastic force and restraint can cause liability, there are equal legal dangers by not taking prompt action or totally controlling the patient.

A patient may show extreme agitation and combativeness one moment and suddenly quiet down. Believing the patient to be in control, the EMS personnel avoids use of restraints only to find the patient later causing unexpected and sudden injury to himself or others. When a patient's self-induced injury is due to the emergency care provider's neglect in using necessary restraints, the patient himself can claim damages. Certainly, an equally strong case can be made by onlookers or even other EMS personnel who undergo avoidable injury.

EMS personnel have the legal responsibility not only to protect the patient from self-inflicted injury but to equally protect persons who could possibly be injured by the patient.

This, too, creates a fine line between using enough force to protect, and yet not forceful enough to be considered too much. The use of excessive restraints would provide a proper degree of protection and would not be injurious to the patient. What should be avoided is force or physical acts that can actually cause harm or injury to the patient.

Can EMS personnel defend themselves against a combative psychiatric patient? The answer is "yes"; however, the EMS personnel can only use the amount of force necessary for self-defense, and to calm and restrain the patient. This may cause much less of a reaction than would be allowed in a normal "self-defense" case. This is based on the idea that the EMS personnel is competent while the adversary does not have full competence. The EMS personnel also voluntarily accepted and put himself to the situation as part of the job and accepted the associated risks.

EMS personnel do not have the right to seek revenge in a punishing way. You can do whatever is necessary to protect yourself or others, and to control the patient. Any use of physical force beyond that would be questionable.

POLICE AND PHYSICIAN INVOLVEMENT

The proper handling of psychiatric cases requires involving the police and in some instances medical assistance.

When receiving a call for a psychiatric emergency, the EMT should phone for police assistance at the site of the "pick-up." The EMT personnel should not assume that the patient can be controlled because statistics prove that many, if not most patients, are indeed agitated.

The police should be used to physically restrain and control the patient. EMT personnel should delay this activity until the police arrive because they are better trained and equipped to handle the physical needs for restraint. Of course, this will also effectively reduce any liability if a claim of "excessive force" results.

In extreme cases the police officer should be along during transport as further complications could develop during transport or upon delivery to a psychiatric facility. One further advantage to police involvement is to support your conclusion about the patient's mental state and the suspected need for the treatment given. Courts will often accept statements from police to a greater extent than from co-workers employed by the same EMS unit.

Physician involvement usually appears in transfer situations. The physician should warn the EMT of the restraints necessary and what may be expected from the patient. It is the physician's responsibility to provide the EMT with proper transport instructions; however, there is an equal obligation on the part of the EMT to get this information.

In some cases a physician will be along during transfer. Physician attendance may be called for when the patient is undergoing extensive drug therapy, or when the patient is of a mind to respond more favorably to the physician. EMT personnel should pass all medical matters to the attending physician, and the EMT's role would be to assist in the treatment, although the EMT would equally share the responsibility of controlling and restraining the patient.

PROTECTION AGAINST FALSE ACCUSATIONS

Frequently, emotionally disturbed patients file unfounded accusations against EMS personnel, especially EMTs.

A patient alone in an ambulance with one attendant can create countless stories of what happened in that ambulance and, unfortunately, it becomes the word of the EMT versus a psychotic patient. There are unlimited cases of female patients (of all ages) referring to sexual misconduct. Other patients say they faced physical abuse and injury. Still others imagine a wide variety of medical misdeeds. The only protection EMT personnel have against the groundless accusation is the evidence of a third party in attendance.

Many EMT units have a standing policy that there be at least two attendants present (in addition to the driver) on all psychiatric case runs. Others require a police officer or other observer to be in attendance during transport. This is an excellent policy and should be followed by all EMTs. It not only makes sure that there are enough personnel to handle the psychiatric emergency, but also prevents any unfounded or distorted allegations.

EMT LIABILITY FOR INVOLUNTARY COMMITMENT

Whether a patient can be placed in a psychiatric unit against his or her will depend to some degree on the laws of your state, but governed by basic principles recently established by the United States Supreme Court. According to the United States Supreme Court cases, involuntary commitment can only occur when the patient is a danger to himself or others. This would include homicidal or suicidal tendencies, although a lesser degree of possible injury may justify commitment.

Basically, the test closely follows that of whether the EMT had the right to forcibly treat and transport the patient without consent in the first instance. The degree to which a psychiatric facility can legally hold a patient, once committed, falls beyond the range of this book and does not legally concern the EMT. However, patients believing they have been illegally committed commonly sue the EMT unit starting the emergency service, as well as the psychiatric facility.

If the EMT can show a reasonable basis for believing the patient represented a danger to himself or others, he or she will have no liability even if more extensive psychiatric determinations find this not to be the case and the patient is released.

Even if an EMT cannot convince a court that his or her judgment was accurate, the patient may be able to press a technical claim of "battery" or "false imprisonment" but without physical injury what would the patient's damages be? Most courts would demand small damages to make up for what amounts to a reasonably brief loss of personal freedom.

However, if the EMT wrongfully decides not to treat an emotionally disturbed patient and the patient later injures himself or others, the final legal award can be large.

This is one reason legal advisors generally recommend forced treatment for the emotionally ill. All factors being equal, it is the most just position and the one least likely to cause serious legal complications.

A TEN-POINT CHECKLIST FOR HANDLING THE EMOTIONALLY DISTURBED PATIENT

1. Call ahead to make sure the police will be there.

2. Use enough personnel to restrain the patient.

3. Document your observations about the patient and why you believe the patient is a danger to himself or others.

4. Try to get consent from a relative, but do not delay needed treatment if quick aid is needed.

5. Keep bystanders and onlookers away from the patient as they may agitate the patient and cause injury.

6. Allow the police to restrain the patient, but never allow more force to be used than is absolutely necessary.

7. Make certain the patient is adequately restrained so he or she cannot inflict injury to himself or others.

8. Require two attendants to be in attendance during transport to make sure of the treatment and properly secure the patient.

9. Provide the ED with the needed information and observations, but avoid slanderous remarks. Limit your record to observations not medical conclusions.

10. Keep the patient's condition confidential.

TEST YOUR KNOWLEDGE

1. How would you determine whether a patient was "emotionally disturbed" to the point where he or she could not legally grant or withhold consent?

2. Can you provide treatment and transport to an emotionally disturbed patient who is not in need of immediate emergency care and presents no harm to himself or others?

3. Under what circumstances is it legal to restrain, force treatment, and transport an emotionally disturbed patient?

4. What degree of force can an EMT use on a combative, emotionally disturbed patient?

5. Under what circumstances can an emotionally disturbed patient be committed against his will to a hospital?

6. What responsibility does an EMT have in protecting bystanders from an emotionally disturbed patient?

9

LAW ENFORCEMENT IN EMERGENCY CARE

As crime rates show a steady rise, EMS personnel can expect an even larger percentage of their calls to be for crime-related incidents. This places an even further responsibility on you as an emergency provider. Beyond the basic function of providing medical care, you have an equal obligation to cooperate with law enforcement agencies.

PATIENT VERSUS POLICE RIGHTS

Due to their position, EMS personnel must walk a fine line between the rights of the patient possibly involved in a crime, and the police who are basically interested in gathering evidence and making an arrest. This may create a possible conflict between you and the police. The police may try to delay or avoid medical treatment, or at least hinder the treatment being carried out in a competent manner while they carry out their law enforcement duties.

Consider these common events:

- Police may demand custody of a patient and demand on taking the patient to a police station, not an ED or hospital, even though the patient needs emergency medical care.

- Police may try to control the patient's treatment by ordering immediate transfer to a hospital without giving the EMT adequate opportunity to examine the patient.

- Police may remove patients from vehicles without proper medical evaluation.

- Police may question patients and search clothing and the body of the patient before letting medical treatment be started, or while treatment is being administered.

This presents an important problem, but one not clearly solved through past cases. Who is in the controlling position, the EMT attempting to give aid or the police?

The police have broad legal authority to enforce the law. They also have the equal right to control a situation to the degree that it does not needlessly hinder emergency care. Police can have vehicles towed or removed from the scene; they can order onlookers to go away; they can question witnesses and gather evidence; and they also have the right to make arrests and hold patients.

The role of EMS personnel is more limited. They only have the authority to give aid. Police should not hinder EMS personnel giving aid because this is the main responsibility of EMS personnel. As the above example demonstrates, however, the spheres of responsibility may overlap and create confusion over the mutual rights of the EMT and the police.

From a strict, legal standpoint the police appear to have the upper hand. Unlawful hindering with police work, even though medically justified, may result in charges of obstruction of justice against the EMS personnel or being a disorderly person, or a similar violation depending on the provisions of state law. Courts are understandably reluctant to permit any hindering of police work, even if the police activities are harmful to the patient from a medical viewpoint.

This does not mean that patients may not have rights against the police should unjustified police action cause further medical harm. A patient has the right to start a negligence claim against the police or a claim for violation of civil rights. However, these rights belong to the patient not EMS personnel. EMS personnel cannot readily defend against a charge of hindering with police work by claiming the rights used by the patient. Perhaps all EMS personnel can do when faced with police demands that hinder emergency care is to seek a practical solution.

Police may let EMS personnel perform their work unhampered if police understand the reason and need for treatment, and are sure that the treatment will not delay them from their rights to enforce the law. However, this is more of an educational and cooperative process, instead of one where the EMT tries to maintain his or her role over the police.

If a conflict should exist between you and the police, follow these guidelines:

1. Meet with the police in private and try to agree on an approach that will satisfy the police needs along with your own. The one major reason for disagreement is lack of communication.

2. Explain to the police why the treatment is needed, and how police work may hinder with the treatment. The police may not be aware of the patient's condition, or the need for treatment, unless you tell them.

3. If the police still refuse to let you start treatment, advise the police diplomatically that you will have to note the incident

and the police action in the trip report. This not only protects you from a later patient claim, but it warns the police that your report may be used against them in any claim by the patient.

4. Listen to the police. They also have a duty to perform and just as your work may be misunderstood by them, the reverse is also true.

5. If you cannot reach an agreement with the police, you must give in to their demands. Continue to perform the treatment allowed by the police and never abandon the patient or do less than the police allow. Some treatment is better than no treatment at all.

6. You are not required to perform services or treatment demanded by the police. They can prevent treatment or even demand you leave the patient and the scene of the accident; however, they cannot order you to take part in an activity harmful to the patient.

7. You can advise the patient about limits placed on treatment by the police. This procedure should be followed so the patient knows that you have done everything possible under the circumstances.

8. Keep a complete and detailed record of the incident. Note all discussions with the police so the record is complete.

In preparing this book, I thought it would be worthwhile to get the views of police who deal with EMTs to discover the problems they have run into. Questioning fifteen police officers, their most common criticism included:

• Undue delay by EMTs in carrying out treatment. They report that many of the tests appear unnecessary and needlessly tie up traffic or prevent a quick handling of the case.

• Lack of communication. Less experienced police officers admit they do not know about EMS procedures, and that they are not given enough information about a patient's condition or the need for treatment.

• Hindering with police work is another common complaint. Examples ranged from disturbing evidence to getting involved in police questioning without being asked to.

These problems will probably continue to exist between police and EMS until both develop the knowledge and appreciation of the other's role.

YOUR OBLIGATIONS AT THE SCENE OF A CRIME

First Responders, and even EMTs, may arrive at the scene of a violent crime before the police arrive. This requires an understanding by EMS personnel of law enforcement in preserving, collecting, and using evidence. Without going into the details of forensic medicine which is beyond the range of this book, it may be enough to state that anything at the scene may provide valuable clues and evidence for the police.

The recommended procedures to follow at the scene of a violent crime include:

1. Immediately notify the police, or call your dispatcher to do so.

2. If the victim is obviously dead, then he or she should remain undisturbed. Even the position of the body can provide valuable clues.

3. Do not touch, move, or relocate any item at the scene unless absolutely necessary to provide treatment to an injured victim. You should mark the location of any item that must be moved so the police can determine its original position.

4. Do not let onlookers or other unauthorized personnel on the premises of the crime scene.

5. Observe and note anything unusual, especially if the evidence may not be present when the police arrive. This may include smoke and odors.

6. Give immediate care to the patient. The fact that the patient is a probable crime victim should not delay prompt treatment. Remember, your role is to provide emergency care, not law enforcement or detective work.

7. Keep detailed records of the incident including your observations of the victim and the scene of the crime. In many felony cases, First Responders and paramedics will be called to testify since they were first on the scene, and lack of records about the case can be professionally embarrassing.

8. Once the police arrive you should leave or at least not hinder their work; however, you should give them any information you believe would be useful.

FORCED RESTRAINT ON SUSPECTS

It is not a common situation, but EMS personnel may be forced into a situation where they come into contact with crime suspects trying to leave a crime scene to avoid being caught.

- A patient may try to leave when the police arrive.
- An uninjured accomplice may try to run from the scene.
- A patient under custody may try to escape through transport to a hospital.

What is the correct action by EMS under each of these situations? The law does not require an agreement to act on the part of EMS personnel to forcibly hold or capture a suspect. The one exception are police First Responders whose duties cover their being law enforcement officers in addition to their EMS role. Even though a patient may be a suspect in a crime, or may have committed a crime in your presence, you are not required to help in forcing restraint upon the suspect.

From a strict legal viewpoint, you can be liable if you do force restraint, even if it is for providing necessary treatment. The one exception may be the patient who does not have the mental capacity to grant consent and he or she requires emergency treatment. Even in this situation you can only use the reasonable restraints necessary to give treatment and not the excessive force required for legal restraint.

EMS personnel often ask about their rights to make a citizen's arrest. The rights of non-law enforcement personnel to make an arrest and forcibly hold a suspect will depend on the laws of the state. Some jurisdictions have specific statutes allowing for citizen's arrest, while others rely on common law principles.

EMS personnel should carefully review the operative laws of their state; however, in most instances the requirements for a valid citizen's arrest are:

1. The suspect committed the crime in the presence of the citizen, or the citizen had reason to believe that the suspect was involved in and is leaving the scene of the crime.
2. The crime, or suspected crime, involved a felony rather than a misdemeanor.
3. The suspect would otherwise leave the scene, continue the commission of the crime, or otherwise avoid arrest.

The problem with "citizen's arrests" by EMS personnel is that an arrest not legally justified can result in a suit for battery, false arrest, and/or false imprisonment. The practical angles are perhaps of even greater importance. To what degree can an unarmed and untrained individual effectively force restraint without potentially causing himself and bystanders grave danger?

Pointing out these legal and practical pitfalls is not intended to discourage intervention by EMS personnel, but rather to caution them that should they elect to make a citizen's arrest, they should first:

- be totally familiar with the state law granting them that authority.
- be certain that they can accomplish the arrest without danger to themselves or others.

Insuring continued custody of the suspect undergoing ambulance transport to a hospital is the basic function of the police. Many municipalities use police transport for this purpose. When private ambulance services are used, the police should decide on the manner of restraint and accompany the EMT. Basically, the EMT should limit himself to treatment, while the police should control the patient to prevent escape or harm to others.

In many instances EMS personnel run into situations where a patient may be involved in a "non-violent" crime or a misdemeanor. This would include patients who are involved in automobile accidents resulting from intoxication, or patients who are under the influence of drugs or have illegal drugs in their possession. In these instances a citizen's arrest would not be called for. EMS personnel may use reasonable efforts to restrain the patient for medical reasons, but any greater use of force would be a cause for a lawsuit.

REPORTING POSSIBLE VIOLATIONS OF LAW

Although EMS personnel have strict limits on their legal rights to arrest or hold a crime suspect, they have an important responsibility to report possible law violations.

EMS personnel are in a rare position to observe the existence of evidence that could mean criminal wrongdoing. It may be drugs in the possession of a patient, concealed weapons, or other forms of illegal material.

This raises the question of whether it is permissible for EMS personnel to report the incident to the police. Many EMS personnel believe that they hold a position of trust over the patient, and the reporting of evidence to the police is a breach of trust or patient-provider confidentiality.

There have been no reported cases where a court forced the responsibility on EMS personnel not to give information. On the other hand, EMS personnel can be liable for not reporting certain incidents to the police. It is possible that an EMT who sees a store of heroin on a patient, and does not report it to the police, may be criminally liable for obstruction of justice, or as an accessory to the crime.

There are instances where evidence may indicate criminal activity, but without any reasonable degree of certainty. An elderly patient may have an unmarked vial of drugs in her possession, but there may be a legal basis for its existence. Reporting the incident to the police could make the EMT a defendant in a defamation of character suit if the reporting was not reasonable or in good faith.

Most states describe the circumstances when reporting is demanded. These commonly include:

- wounds by gunshot (some states extend this to include knife wounds)
- rape incidents
- attempted suicide cases
- drug overdoses and poisoning
- child abuse cases
- unlawful possession or using of controlled drugs

Under the reporting statutes the obligation to report may rest with the ED or physicians rather than be forced upon other EMS personnel. Therefore, a review should be made of the applicable laws to determine who must report what.

First Responder units, and EMTs through their ambulance services, should establish a reporting policy that follows state law and have a cooperative working relationship with the police. This written policy should be part of the policy and procedures manual, and strictly followed.

The method for reporting suspicious evidence or situations should also be part of the policy. In many instances, the report is verbal and this is justified when prompt action is needed to seize evidence, but this should still be followed up by a written notice.

Although the report should meet with statutory requirements, it is equally important that EMS personnel not provide conclusions that are unjustified. If a drug is seen, you should limit your report to the physical description of the drug rather than concluding what it is.

The written report serves two purposes:

1. It documents the fact that you did report, and
2. It defines precisely what you are reporting.

This record can protect you from police or patient action in the future.

EMS personnel involved in a crime-related incident should avoid issuing any comments to the news media. This is beyond the area of EMS responsibilities and can lead to an action for invasion of privacy or slander, whether the report is true or not. Further, any statements made can be used to disagree with you at the time of trial should you be needed to testify.

Reporting needs do not force EMS personnel to seize or take custody of the evidence. A patient may attempt to hide drugs in a body cavity, or get rid of possible evidence such as a gun, drugs, or burglary tools.

To the degree that the hiding of drugs on the person does not hinder medical treatment, you should avoid any attempt to remove or take possession of the item, but instead notify the police. Any attempt to take the item from the patient can be considered technical "battery" of the patient, and even more important, the item may lose its value as evidence due to improper seizure. The grounds on which police can search and seize evidence from a patient remain the same as for any other crime suspect. Due to the technicalities involved in conducting a search and seizure, it is best left to the police.

YOUR OBLIGATION TO TESTIFY

The testimony of the EMS personnel who can provide an "eyewitness" report to the circumstances surrounding either a crime-related injury or arrest, can be vital to either the prosecution or the defense. Prosecutors may rely on EMS personnel to testify on or support:

- the condition of the victim or suspect.
- identification of evidence (weapons, drugs, or other items).
- the procedure followed by police in making the arrest or seizing evidence.
- incriminating admissions or confessions made by the suspect.
- facts or observations relating to the crime scene.

On the other hand, defense counsel may want your testimony to deny any accusations of the prosecution or to testify about your observations that would make a search and seizure, confession, or arrest illegal.

Your involvement as a witness may be limited to one small point of disagreement or you may be a "key" witness on whose testimony the case will either succeed or fail. EMS personnel can be forced to testify and produce their records through the issuing of a subpoena. Your presence as a witness can be called for by the prosecution or the defense. In many cases your presence as a witness will be voluntarily at the request of a prosecutor, and it is generally good policy to let the police know you will cooperate and testify without the need for a subpoena.

In a typical criminal case, you may be required to testify several times. Your first appearance may be before a grand jury who will decide whether there is enough evidence to formally charge the defendant with a crime by issuing an indictment. The police may file a complaint against the defendant to start criminal proceedings and shortly after this the court will hold a "probable cause" hearing to decide whether there is enough evidence for the complaint. Even where there is "probable cause" the prosecutor may later give the case to a grand jury if the crime is serious. Following these procedures the case will go to trial on its merits and again you will be asked to testify. Your role during these proceedings is only that of a witness. This means you are neutral, even though your testimony may be helpful to the prosecution or the defense.

As a professional called upon to provide essential evidence, you should follow these guidelines:

1. Never discuss the case with outsiders or reporters.

2. Keep detailed records of the incident. Your records will usually be subpoenaed and used to back up your testimony. Further, you have the right to look at your records to refresh your memory on the situation if your records were kept in the ordinary course of business. Records that are incomplete or do not follow your testimony can damage both your credibility as a witness and your professional reputation.

3. Truth is the one necessity in all testimony. State your observations as you honestly recall them. Do not allow the prosecution or the defense to change your testimony, as long as you believe that your testimony is truthful.

4. Testify only to what you know or have personally observed. If you do not remember an item say so. No witness can be expected to clearly remember every detail of a situation months or years after the fact.

5. Stay reliable in your testimony unless a change in prior testimony is justified. What you say at a trial will be compared to what you have stated at a probable cause or grand jury proceeding.

6. Remain calm when testifying. If you are called as a government witness you should expect a strong cross-examination by the defense, and the reverse would also be true. This is all part of the adversary process and you will have nothing to worry about, providing you answer completely and honestly.

TEST YOUR KNOWLEDGE

1. Can the police prevent you from treating or transporting a patient in medical need?

2. Can the police force you to give aid to a patient or tell you the manner of treatment?

3. What steps should you take if police prevent treatment or transport of a patient requiring emergency care?

4. Under what circumstances, if any, can you forcibly restrain a patient trying to leave the scene of a crime or accident to avoid being caught by police?

5. What are the dangers in assisting police who administer blood-alcohol tests at the scene of an accident?

6. Do you have the duty to report concealed weapons, drugs, or other evidence of illegal activity under your state's law?

7. Do you have the right to forcibly remove and take possession of illegal items hidden on a patient?

8. What role may your records play in a criminal prosecution?

9. Can you leave a patient if the police delay treatment and transport until they question the patient?

10

SPECIAL CARE SITUATIONS

Every emergency case has a special set of facts, and needs its own set of facts to provide the best response. However, there are certain cases that demand not only an awareness of the proper medical treatment, but a complete understanding of the legal responsibilities as well. In this chapter we will take a closer look at some of the most frequently encountered situations and center on the legal angles necessary to avoid liability.

HANDLING THE DYING OR DECEASED PATIENT

EMS personnel are often the last persons to see a dying person alive. The patient may realize that death is near, whether from a terminal disease or an accident, and still be conscious and even able to communicate.

Your closeness to the dying patient places certain legal requirements on you because you may be the last person to receive information meant to be communicated to others.

Dying patients may rely upon you to:

1. Tell relatives or friends about the distribution or location of property and hidden valuables.

2. Deliver an important message to a friend or relative. Normally, the dying patient saves his or her innermost thoughts until the time of death.

3. Deliver to a friend or relative a valuable piece of jewelry, heirloom, or other item with the aim to make the item a gift. Giving you the item to give to the friend or relative means the gift belongs to that person.

4. Advise relatives of the patient's last-minute wishes about burial instructions.

5. Tell law enforcement authorities any "dying declarations." A dying declaration may be an admission to a crime or a statement denying past testimony given against another person. Dying declarations can be used as evidence because they are statements against the interest of the patient and made in the face of death. Therefore, the law attaches a view of truth to the statement even though the patient can no longer prove it.

In any of the above situations, what you hear can be of vital importance to the patient, his or her friends or relatives, law enforcement agencies, and even other persons wrongfully convicted of a crime. The degree to which these people will benefit from the statements of the deceased will depend on your ability to communicate his or her final statements.

EMS personnel attending a dying patient must:

• Listen carefully to what the patient is saying. It may not appear important at the time, especially in regard to the medical crisis. However, it may have significance to the patient or others and the importance of the message may not be recognized until a later date.

• Record the message. Maintain detailed notes and be certain that you record the message completely and accurately. In the case of a dying declaration, the value of the message from the viewpoint as evidence will depend on how clear it is.

• Communicate the message. Immediately notify the closest relatives of the message, and in the case of dying declarations, these must be reported to the authorities. It is considered obstruction of justice and withholding of evidence if you do not report this information.

• Retain confidentiality. Aside from communicating what was meant to be communicated to friends or relatives, or the necessary reporting of incriminating dying declarations to the authorities, you should keep secret any final statements, particularly if they can be of no constructive benefit to the receiver.

On occasion you may respond to transport a critially ill or injured patient only to find that he or she died before your arrival. If the patient is dead you still have the legal obligation to transport the patient and provide emergency care services according to the patient's condition.

The reason for this is that you cannot legally make the determination of death. Death in most jurisdictions can only be legally pronounced by a physician, medical examiner, or coroner. Therefore, avoiding or stopping transport or treatment to a patient believed dead does not conform to the role of EMS personnel who are obligated to continue doing everything possible to maintain or revive life, until a death certificate is made.

The clear legal danger in stating that death has occurred and terminating life support treatment is that the patient, through his or her estate, may later claim that the cause of death was caused by failure to act, or that his or her life may have been saved by prompt and continuous action. It may not be true, but you will be in a weak legal position to justify your non-action because you cannot establish that the patient was dead and, therefore, no longer in need of emergency care.

Broaden this problem to cover the patient who is obviously dead (decapitated, charred by burning, extensive gunshot wounds) to the point where no reasonable person could reach any other conclusion. Does an EMT still have to transport and treat? As a practical matter there would be no basis for a claim as the question of the patient's prior death is apparent to the point where no rational person could raise it. However, even in these situations an EMT should provide immediate transport to the hospital, so the patient can be certified as DOA ("dead on arrival").

If the patient is obviously dead and appears to be the victim of a crime, it is wise to avoid transport because touching or transporting the victim may destroy valuable evidence for the police. The position of the body, body temperature (an important fact in determining time of death), and even microscopic fibers or other evidence lodged on the body would be lost to police investigators. Frequently an EMT will answer an emergency only to find a physician present and the patient certified as dead. As a legal matter, this terminates your responsibility; however, as a professional you should remain and offer whatever assistance the physician may require.

When death is from natural causes, the physician or a relative may arrange for transport by a funeral director. In accident cases, or where the person died of unknown or suspicious causes, an autopsy may be required and this will require transport to a hospital or municipal mortuary. You may be requested to transport the deceased patient to either a funeral home or a hospital, particularly when there is no other means of transport immediately available. Unless an EMT is assigned to a coroner's office or has a contractual duty to transport deceased patients, the EMT may legally refuse to do so, although as a professional you should not refuse without good reason.

CHILD ABUSE CASES

Child abuse cases are among the most tragic in emergency care. They represent a special challenge to EMTs because they are probably in the best position to determine whether a child abuse case exists. The ED may be in a better position to diagnose the child's physical condition, but the EMT may be the one to see how the parents act, or the background that would lead to the conclusion that the injury to the child was done on purpose rather than accidental.

Child abuse is defined as a case where a minor suffers serious physical injury that is performed on purpose, not by accidental means. Child abuse can take a variety of means and may be abuse over a long period due to severe neglect.

Every state has a child abuse reporting requirement placed on the hospital staff attending to an abused child. This is where the role of the EMT becomes important. Although the statutes place the balance of reporting on the hospital rather than on EMTs, the EMT should still inform the ED of any facts or observations that would help the hospital in deciding whether a child abuse case may exist and whether a report and investigation is needed.

For example, a child may be admitted to a hospital for head injuries. The ED may be told by the child's parents that the injury was accidental; however, the EMT may have seen a blood-stained weapon on the scene when responding to the call, or may have heard conflicting statements about the cause of the injury. Given this information the hospital may begin to detect that the injury was not due to accidental means.

State laws protect emergency care personnel who file a child abuse report if it is determined after investigating that no child abuse exists. The only requirement placed on emergency care personnel to get immunity is that the report be made in "good faith" and upon "reasonable belief" that the child may have been abused.

Do not assume that ED personnel will detect a child abuse case without your help. Your main duty is to provide emergency care to the battered or abused child. You are not obligated to be a detective to uncover all the facts leading to the injury. That does not mean that you should close your eyes to the problem. Tell the ED when you believe a child has been abused and keep a record of your observations and the notification.

In some child abuse cases the call for assistance is made by a neighbor or onlooker who sees the abuse. When arriving at the scene the EMT may be faced with a child in obvious need for aid and a parent who refuses aid or transport for the child. Without parental consent an EMT should not attempt to forcibly remove the child; however, the EMT can take reasonable steps to protect the child from further physical danger. In this situation the EMT should phone for police assistance and stand by to administer aid only after the police have acted on the case and placed the child with the EMT for treatment and transport.

THE RAPE AND SEXUALLY ABUSED PATIENT

Patients believed to be the victims of rape or sexual abuse place certain legal obligations on EMTs. Many EMTs see the rape victim as a person needing medical treatment with little concern for the legal bearings in handling the case. In truth, the rape case can place liability on the EMT who ignores the delicate legal issues that the rape case presents.

The first legal concern involves the treatment given to the rape victim. Your main goal must be to comfort and reassure the patient, and to provide only essential treatment, while saving the patient's physical condition for examination and detection of evidence to support a rape accusation.

To accomplish this goal you should:

1. Reassure the patient. Introduce yourself and your title. The patient has just gone through a horrifying experience and she must gain confidence in you.

2. Inspect the patient's garments and general medical condition. Note any outer or visual signs of physical assault.

3. Ask about her physical condition or the medical aid she may require. Do not question her about the rape incident as this is a police duty.

4. Do not examine or touch the patient's body unless absolutely necessary. Your physical handling of the patient can bring back her shock of the incident.

5. Get the patient to consent to whatever treatment you do give. Make sure she understands what you want to do and that she agrees to accept it.

6. Avoid examination or treatment of the genital area. This may go against accepted medical practice, but any disturbance or cleansing of the genital area can remove semen or other evidence needed to prove the rape case. Aside from the considerations to save evidence, immediate examination or treatment of this area of the body can be disturbing to a patient and should be left to ED personnel unless immediate care is required.

7. Do not let the patient wash herself, urinate, or defecate until she is medically examined and all evidence is gotten from her body.

8. Transport the victim to a chosen treatment center for sexual

assault. Not every hospital is prepared to handle rape cases so the EMT should know in advance where to go.

When these procedures are carefully followed the patient has gotten all the medical assistance needed at the EMT level, and of equal importance the EMT has saved the evidence required.

The second consideration to think about in handling a rape patient is to avoid accusations that you acted improperly. It is understandable why it is statistically true that the greatest number of wrongful accusations against EMTs come from rape victims. Rape often brings on emotional hysteria, hostility, and distrust. EMTs involved in this situation must act with extreme caution to avoid being the target of emotionally caused accusations.

There have been instances of rape victims accusing EMTs of physical abuse and even molestation. The EMT can only guard against this possibility by avoiding physical contact with the patient and having a second EMT, police officer, or some other person accompany the patient during transport.

A few states require that rape cases be reported; however, most states leave the decision to report a rape to the patient. Those few states that do require reporting place the obligation on the attending physician or ED, not on other EMS personnel.

Keeping information hidden is critical in a rape case. It is the one type of case where a patient may be able to claim large damages through the emotional trauma of having the incident publicized without the patient's consent. Newspapers have a policy of not releasing a rape patient's name to protect the patient from what she may see as social embarrassment.

As with other felony-related cases, your records should detail any information provided by the patient, even if it is about the crime itself rather than her medical condition. The patient may describe the assailant, or any other memory she may have about the incident. Normally, a patient will not remember the incident in so much detail at a later time, and the EMT's records can be useful in recalling specific angles of the crime.

The law is not clear on whether an EMT can give information to the police without consent from the patient. Most legal authorities would agree with the conclusion that no liability would exist in such a situation, although there are cases that say EMS personnel cannot give information to relatives, clergy, or even rape crisis centers without patient consent. The prudent policy to follow is to get the patient's consent before any information is passed out.

Rape cases require a large amount of delicacy and knowledge about the handling of patients in emotional crises. Most lawsuits result from the EMT not bringing his or her needed skill to the situation.

Dispatchers should take this into consideration when assigning EMTs to a rape call.

THE ALCOHOL INTOXICATED PATIENT

A very high percentage of accident-related injuries are caused by alcohol intoxication. This is true not only of automobile accidents but household and "on the job" injuries. The intoxicated patient imposes the following legal problems on EMS personnel.

- The patient may resist treatment and attempt to leave the scene of the accident.
- Police may try to arrest or conduct examinations to determine the level of intoxication. This evidence may then be used to prosecute or to take away motor vehicle licenses.
- Motorists involved in an accident with an intoxicated person may rely on the EMT records to prove intoxication.
- The patient may become violent and cause injury to bystanders for which EMS personnel can be held accountable.

Let's take a closer look at each of these potential trouble spots and define the proper legal guidelines to follow.

EMS personnel do not have to get patient consent to treat, if the patient is clearly intoxicated and the patient needs immediate treatment, or may cause further injury to himself or others. In fact, the patient would have a reasonable basis for claiming negligence if you do not give the needed emergency care.

Restraint of the patient should be handled by the police whenever possible. However, if there are no police around you may use whatever force is reasonable to control and calm the patient to the point where treatment and transport is possible. Continued restraint on the patient through the use of restraining belts and blankets should be used if the patient is violent or may become violent. However, physical restraints should be kept to a minimum if the patient responds to conversation.

You have a duty to protect the patient and other bystanders; on the other hand your goal is to provide treatment with the least amount of pressure. How you will achieve that balance should decide your plan of action.

Police have the right to question the patient to decide the state of intoxication, and this is one instance where police work cannot wait because blood-alcohol levels drop with the passage of time. The police may ask the patient to walk, recite the alphabet, or talk to the patient to determine the degree of alcohol intoxication. In some jurisdictions the police will try to take the patient to headquarters for a "breathalyzer" test or a blood sample to determine clinically the blood-alcohol level. In some jurisdictions a breathalyzer test may be done on the roadside. The difficulty with EMS involvement in conducting a breathalyzer or blood test on an intoxicated patient is that the EMS personnel may face liability for battery or violation of civil rights.

In most states patients can refuse to take a breathalyzer or blood test, but they can lose their drivers' licenses as a result. Other states permit a forced breathalyzer or blood test if the patient was driving under the influence of alcohol, but only under these conditions. Some states say consent is given if the patient is unconscious and others hold just the opposite view.

You may be liable if you help the police conduct a breathalyzer or blood test even if your activity is just assisting the police (holding the patient). Since state laws vary widely on the patient's rights under these circumstances, EMS personnel should never take part in a testing procedure without first checking with the law in their state.

In many instances, the police may take the patient into custody when EMS personnel believe the patient needs medical treatment. If this happens, you should tell the police your reasons for recommending hospital transport and treatment. If the police still insist on arresting the patient, you should document your findings and discussion with the police in your records. Police do have the final say in the handling of the patient and EMS personnel should never hinder the rights of the police to take a patient into custody.

EMS personnel do have the duty to thoroughly examine the patient to determine whether the patient is suffering from acute intoxication, or whether there are other or additional medical problems. What may appear as an intoxication case may in reality be anything from epilepsy to emotional disturbance. Abandoning the patient to the police without ruling out other potential illnesses can create liability if the police were not warned that the patient may suffer from an illness other than intoxication.

The condition of the patient may be of interest later to other motorists injured by the patient or even the patient's own insurance company. Your record should avoid any conclusion about the degree of intoxication as you are in no position to determine it clinically.

Your record can explain the general condition of the patient, and what you have observed, but even then the record should avoid needless slang such as "the patient's drunk," "plastered," or other similar unprofessional commentary. It would be correct to say that "the patient has alcohol on his breath," or "the patient cannot maintain a normal conversation." You properly described the patient's condition and what you have observed without risking yourself or the patient with damaging conclusions.

As with all patient records, they are confidential and should not be told to anyone but the patient or the ED, without written patient consent or a valid court subpoena. This nondisclosure policy should be broad enough to equally cover the police and the patient's own motor vehicle insurance underwriter.

Your record will be of greater use to the ED if you can get advance information from the patient. This may include the type and quantity of alcohol consumed, drugs the patient may be taking, and existing diseases and medical disorders. When immediate ED treatment is needed, this information can speed up treatment, and reduce the liability as it documents the evaluation you made of the patient's condition.

SUICIDE CASES

Suicide cases follow many of the same procedures used with emotionally disturbed patients discussed in Chapter 8. However, suicide cases have a further dimension: The patient has attempted to take his or her life and may try again. This also places additional legal duties on EMS personnel.

Consent to treat suidical patients is not needed because they do not have the mental capacity to give consent and treatment is required under the "Emergency Doctrine." You may use whatever force is reasonably needed to restrain the patient for needed transport and treatment. Restraint during transport is vital because the EMT can be held liable for any further self-inflicted injury to the patient that should have been reasonably predicted and avoided.

Most suicide attempts are tried using poisons or drug overdoses. EMS personnel have the main duty to find out what poison or drug was used so that a proper antidote can be used by the ED without delay. Often the drug will be a common prescription item (barbiturates or other tranquilizers or sedatives) not identified by name. EMTs should phone the ED with identifying characteristics of the drug or poison, as the ED will often have to spend valuable time trying to identify the drug so that an antidote can be used. A patient could bring a negligence action against an EMT who fails to take the necessary action to coordinate treatment with the ED. Some states require that suicide cases be reported to the police. Those states generally place the burden to report on the emergency physician rather than on the EMT or paramedic.

EMT reports should not classify the death or attempt as a suicide if there are other possible causes. Often a patient may accidentally overdose on sedatives with no thought of committing suicide. A report mentioning "suicide" in such an instance would not be legally justified and could cause the patient to lose life insurance benefits.

ANIMAL BITE CASES

EMTs and other emergency care responders have a limited, but clearly defined, responsibility in cases involving animal bites. Most states have public health laws that make it a duty to take reasonable steps to get the carcass of the animal, or to at least get identification of the animal if it is a household pet. Unlike ED personnel, EMTs generally do get close to the animal or can at least get a description of the animal from bystanders or relatives, if not from the patient.

It is important to identify the animal so it can be captured quickly by police or animal wardens, and to later test the animal for rabies. EMTs do not have the responsibility to capture the animal, but they should take the animal into custody if at all possible. In most cases the EMT's duties will have been carried out by getting whatever information possible about the description and location of the animal, and communicating this information to the police, animal warden, and the ED personnel.

Handling special care situations involves more than knowledge of the specific legal obligations and problems they present. As with all emergency care cases, they need prompt and proper medical treatment to give the patient what he or she has the right to expect—total competence and professionalism on the part of EMS personnel.

TEST YOUR KNOWLEDGE

1. What is meant by a "dying declaration?"
2. Under what circumstances can you avoid treatment or transport to a patient believed dead?
3. Why is it important to maintain life-sustaining treatment to a patient with no vital signs and thought to be dead?
4. Does your state require you to report child abuse cases?
5. What should an EMT do if he or she responds to a child abuse call and the parents resist treatment or transport of the child?
6. What treatment should be given to a rape patient, and to save the evidence needed to save a rape case?
7. Does a suicide patient have enough mental capacity to refuse consent?

11

OBSERVING RECORD-KEEPING REQUIREMENTS

In recent years record keeping by EMS personnel has taken on a major legal importance.

The traditional records of years ago did little more than tell the name of the patient, date of service, and destination. The record's main purpose was to document that an emergency call was made and little else.

Today, EMS personnel face strict record-keeping requirements. In many states, record-keeping requirements are enforced by state regulations. Third party reimbursement plans have their own needs, and most important, proper records are needed to send vital information to emergency departments and other health providers.

WHO MAY REVIEW YOUR RECORDS

Modern EMS records are used to document the information needed by everyone associated with the EMS system.

- Emergency departments may use EMS records to get a history of the accident, original condition, and prior treatment of the patient. Therefore, the EMS record becomes that "all important" first record that other health professionals will use to decide on further treatment.

- As an operational record, municipalities and ambulance services are relying more on data obtained from records to judge response times, efficiency of service, and the costs of operation. The EMS record serves as a basic management tool to create a more efficient and "cost justified" EMS system.

- From a monetary viewpoint, the EMS record will provide the data needed to complete billing forms under a wide range and number of billing programs—including Medicare, Medicaid, Blue Cross-Blue Shield, and other insurance coverages. In this measure, the EMS record becomes the basis for all accounts receivable billing.

- As court evidence, the EMS record is often very important. The condition of a patient at the time of the accident may be in question when a defendant is challenging a damage claim. A defense may be based on intoxication of the other party. Your records may indicate this condition existed. Anything you see and record can have legal importance in the courtroom, whether it be a simple civil suit or a criminal proceeding. With increasing frequency, the EMT's observations and records are used in the litigation process.

- EMT records may also be helpful to police and other law enforcement personnel. Your records may contain valuable information about child abuse or rape cases, or to record "dying declarations," the disposal of patient's valuables, or other evidence useful to either the estate of a deceased party or to police involving death by questionable means.

- Other law enforcement and governmental agencies will also depend on accurate records maintained by you. Cases involving accidental or sudden death may have to be forwarded to the coroner or medical examiner to determine the cause of death. Frequently, EMT records are asked for in these situations. Injury from animal bites or sickness caused by contagious disease may require that an EMT's records by given to a community health officer. Even environmental affairs departments are increasingly using EMT records to document cases of injuries caused by toxic waste, pollution, radiation, or chemicals. As you can see, there is no shortage of people and agencies who use your records to help them in their own work.

From your own viewpoint, however, whether you are an EMT/ Paramedic or First Responder, the record has a special importance. If you are faced with a malpractice suit, your records, if properly kept, can explain what you did for the patient and why. The record becomes your "justification" of services provided—or not provided. Therefore, the record can be valuable evidence in your hands or in the hands of the patient's attorney, depending on how those records were kept.

DEVELOPING PROPER RECORD-KEEPING TECHNIQUES

Even the most casual physician is very sensitive to the need for careful documentation or record keeping. Today, all but the most daring health practitioners keep a carefully constructed record show-ing all related information about a patient's condition and treatment. Certainly, this is only good medical practice; however, physicians and other health practitioners know that it is also a "must" from a malpractice viewpoint.

Hauled into court years later to justify their action, the complete record is all that stands between physicians and a plaintiff's attorney stating that the physician was in one way or another negligent. If the record sticks to the facts, it can be used by the physician to refresh his or her memory to recall the facts and to defend his or her position. Physicians and other health professionals have learned to keep records that can legally stand on their own to properly explain a course of conduct.

Many EMTs have not yet recognized the importance properly maintained records have to discourage or defeat a malpractice claim. All too often, EMS personnel will only record the information re-quired to satisfy the demands of their employer or third-party pay-ment agencies. They give little thought to these records as a written justification of the service provided. This is unfortunate. Without a complete record which is accurate and logical, the EMT has little hope of later defending his or her position because memory alone will not be enough in court, and the EMT can be easily challenged years later when a case goes to trial.

Adequate records are useful in discouraging malpractice cases before they even begin. Often, a plaintiff's attorney will request cop-ies of medical records from all practitioners (including EMTs) in-volved in the patient care. The obvious purpose is to determine which practitioners may have liability.

Providing the patient's attorney with incomplete records, or rec-ords that do not appear to justify the action taken—or not taken, will certainly encourage suing the EMT as a party defendant. The EMT may have a valid defense, and perhaps his or her conduct was proper under the fact pattern; nevertheless, unless the patient's attorney can draw that conclusion from carefully documented records, he or she may well decide some accountability lies with the EMT.

Place yourself in the position of the patient's counsel. He or she knows that you did, or did not, perform a particular service. Perhaps you did not clear an airway and later the patient suffered serious respiratory problems. What do your records show about the condi-tion of the patient and why did you decide that airway clearance was not required? Unless your record shows that you tested the patient for airway blockage and found respiration normal and un-impaired, the attorney can only conclude that you never tested at all—and that was a negligent omission on your part. Even if you did test for airway blockage, how could the patient's attorney know this unless he or she sees it on the record? Your claim that you did test for airway blockage will, or course, be seen as a "self-serving" statement not supported by your own medical record.

Even the best emergency medical care can be taken to be something less once it is reduced to writing. It is never enough to just give quality care. You must document the care so that you do not fall victim to what you neglected to say.

WHAT YOUR RECORDS SHOULD CONTAIN

Record keeping in the emergency care field will vary depending on the level of care. First Responders generally need to keep minimal records. EMTs will need more detailed records, and EMT/paramedics may need even more detailed information due to the more complex nature of their job.

Emergency departments have imposed on them even greater detail and comprehensiveness. Therefore, what would be enough information for one EMS personnel, may not be enough for another.

Most EMT units have developed their own forms. In many instances they are standard within the industry or, as with First Responders, one developed for use within a municipality. In some instances the form is ordered by state regulation.

The form itself is not important. What is important is that it adequately provides the information expected from that level of EMS personnel. The EMS record should as a minimum include the following information.

1. Identification of the EMS vehicle and personnel.
2. Location of the emergency.
3. Call time, date, and response time.
4. Name of the patient(s).
5. Who made the call.
6. The type of injury or accident reported.
7. Patient evaluation by the EMT, including vital signs, skin temperature, colorations, level of consciousness, pupil dilations, and all other relevant physical observations.
8. Relevant medical history of the patient.
9. Rescue and removal information where needed.
10. Treatment given to the patient. This would include oxygen, suction, airway establishment, cervical collars, backboard application, drugs, and any other forms of aid.

11. Destination and arrival time, and condition of the patient at the point of destination if the condition changed.

The record should also contain any information that would be useful in documenting the service.

Many ambulance services use an anatomical outline on their record so the EMT can circle the areas of injury. Every record should have enough space to add related information or to expand on the answers given in the form. Many EMTs conveniently use this space to record:

- Observations of the accident.

- Relevant comments or statements by the patient.

- Refusals to consent to care (a written release should be obtained in this situation).

- Notes about care given by other responders or EMS personnel at the scene.

- Names of bystanders or attenders (friends or relatives who were present during the transport).

Regardless of the form used, it should provide enough opportunity to record in detail all information that is relevant. It is better to say too much than to say too little. Brief reporting can cause more legal complications than excessive reporting.

RECORDING INFORMATION

The amount of detail in your report can greatly influence your liability in a malpractice case. Defense attorneys representing EMS personnel frequently call attention to information that is distorted or wrongfully concluded as a major legal trap. EMS personnel should limit their comments to:

1. What they personally have seen.

2. The conclusions they have the capacity to make as EMS personnel.

For example, it would not be medically justified for an EMS personnel to diagnose "cervical fracture." This diagnosis can only be made at the hospital level. EMS personnel may accurately report the symptoms—paralysis of the extremities or immobilization—because this can be observed.

Intoxication is another example. You can record the presence of alcohol on breath (AOB) and even carry out treatment for intoxication. However, the word "intoxication" defines a medical and legal

AMBULANCE REPORT
Montgomery County-Fire/Rescue Services

COMPLETED BY FIRST DUE UNIT ONLY

LOCATION INFORMATION

A

| 5 0 | Incident No. | Time | Date | Station Run No. | Change ☐ |
| | 1 2 3   7 | Out: In: | | | Delete ☐ |

Incident Type | Action Taken | Occupant
10 11 | ☐ 1 = Ambulance Service
☐ 2 = Rescue/First Aid Only | 12

Address - Location | City
13 | 45

Census Tract | District | Property Classification | Complex | Individual
46   50 | | 51 52 | 53 54 | 55   57

COMPLETE FOR EACH UNIT RESPONDING

UNIT INFO

B

| 6 0 | Incident No. | Suf. | Unit | Assigned Station | Responded From | Disposition | | Transfer Station No. |
| | 1 2 3   7 | 8 9 | 13 | 14 15 | 16 17 | ☐ 11 = In Serv. W/Respond. | ☐ 22 = No Service
☐ 33 = Serv. Rend.
☐ 44 = Serv. Refused | 18 19 |

Unit Operation
☐ 1 = None   ☐ 4 = First-Aid/Rescue   ☐ 7 = Other
☐ 2 = Search/Rescue   ☐ 5 = Investigation
☐ 3 = Extinguishment   ☐ 6 = Ventilation/Salvage

Personnel on Unit
Pd. Vol. / Pd. Vol. / Pd. Vol.
ON UNIT [ ] 20 | AT SC 21 22 23 24 25 26 | AT 6T 27 28 29 30

COMPLETE FOR FIRST PATIENT

PATIENT INFO

C

| 2 0 | Age | Sex | Male (M)
Female (F) | Part of Body Affected | Nature of Illness or Injury |
| | 1 2   14 16 | | 17 | 18 19 | 20 22 |

Treatment Performed | Disposition | Hospital | Transported
23 24 | 25 | 26 27 | Routine (R) or Emergency (E) | 28

ame | | Time | B/P | Pulse | Resp. | Notes
| | / | | | |

Address | | /
| | /

COMPLETE FOR SECOND PATIENT

PATIENT INFO

D

| 2 0 | Age | Sex | Male (M)
Female (F) | Part of Body Affected | Nature of Illness or Injury |
| | 1 2   14 16 | | 17 | 18 19 | 20 22 |

Treatment Performed | Disposition | Hospital | Transported
23 24 | 25 | 26 27 | Routine (R) or Emergency (E) | 28

Name | | Time | B/P | Pulse | Resp. | Notes
| | / | | | |

Address | | /
| | /

E

See Second RS-100 Form (For More Than 2 pts.) ☐ | Unit Commander

Check If MICU Responded ☐ | Incident Commander

RS-100 (Rev. 3-76)

STATION COPY

☐ LYCOMING ☐ SULLIVAN ☐ TIOGA	**AMBULANCE** STANDARD REPORT FORM	MEDICARE NO. DPA NO. MEMBERSHIP NO.

Response No.	Date of Call	How Call Was Received	Ambulance Service	Ambulance No.	

1. Time Information

Ambulance Responding _____

Arrived at Scene _____

Departed Scene _____

Arrived Destination _____

Available For Service _____

2. Address of Incident

HOME/BUSINESS/FACTORY/ETC.   STREET / ROUTE NO.   CITY

3. Patient Information

☐ MALE

LAST NAME   FIRST   M.I.   ☐ FEMALE   AGE

STREET ADDRESS   CITY   STATE   ZIP

4. Patient Taken To:

☐ HOSPITAL
☐ HOME   NAME OF LOCATION
☐ NURSING HOME
☐ PHYSICIAN'S OFFICE   STREET ADDRESS
☐ OTHER   CITY   STATE   ZIP

5. Mileage

_____ IN
_____ OUT
_____ TOTAL

6. Nature of Call

☐ EMERGENCY   ☐ FIRE CALL
☐ URGENT TRANSFER   ☐ STAND-BY
☐ ROUTINE TRANSFER   ☐ NO SERVICE

7. Location of Incident

☐ HIGHWAY   ☐ PUBLIC BLDG.
☐ HOME   ☐ SCHOOL
☐ WORK   ☐ OTHER

8. Medic Alert

☐ NO
☐ YES
☐ TYPE _____

9. Type of Medical Emergency

☐ ABDOMINAL PAINS	☐ DRUGS	☐ PSYCHIATRIC	☐ VOMITING
☐ ABRASIONS	☐ ELECTROCUTION	☐ POISONING	☐ OTHER
☐ BREATHING	☐ FRACTURE	☐ SEIZURE	
☐ BURNS	☐ GUNSHOT	☐ STAB WOUND	
☐ CARDIAC	☐ LACERATIONS	☐ STROKE	
☐ DROWNING	☐ MATERNITY	☐ SUICIDE	

10. Location of Injury

☐ HEAD	☐ ABDOMEN
☐ FACE	☐ ARMS
☐ NECK	☐ HANDS
☐ CHEST	☐ LEGS
☐ BACK	☐ FEET

11. Cause of Injury

Example — Motor Vehicle Accident, Fell From Tree, Gun Shot Wound, Etc.

12. Victim Status

(AT SCENE)
☐ CONSCIOUS
☐ SEMI-CONSCIOUS
☐ UNCONSCIOUS

13. Case Severity

☐ MINOR
☐ SEVERE
☐ CRITICAL

☐ APPARENT DEATH BEFORE ARRIVAL
☐ APPARENT DEATH AFTER ARRIVAL
☐ APPARENT DEATH EN ROUTE
☐ UNKNOWN

14. Care Administered

☐ AIRWAY CONTROL	☐ PSYCHOLOGICAL CARE
☐ BANDAGING	☐ SPINAL IMMOBILIZATION
☐ CPR	☐ SUCTIONING
☐ LIMB SPLINTS	☐ TRANSPORTATION ONLY
☐ OXYGEN	☐ TRACTION
	☐ OTHER _____

15. Vital Signs

	At Scene	En Route
PUPILS		
PULSE		
RESP.		
B.P.	____/____	____/____

16. Condition En Route

☐ IMPROVED
☐ UNCHANGED
☐ WEAKENED
COMMENTS:

17. Release

I refused treatment against the advice of the attendants:

X _____

WITNESSED _____

19. Crew Signature

_____
DRIVER

_____
ATTENDANT

_____
ATTENDANT

EMT ☐

☐

☐

18. Additional Comments, Etc.
Supplies Used / Eq. Left at E.R.

Ambulance Copy   B.M.P., WILLIAMSPORT, PA.

Run No.	CONFIDENTIAL MEDICAL INFORMATION	Date

PATIENT DATA

EMERGENCY CARE RECORD

Printed by Public Health Services. EMS-1304 Project
Portland (Me.) Medical Crisis Unit
Form developed by: J. Clair, R. Devlin, E. Walker

Name _____ last

Address _____

_____ Zip _____ Phone _____

Male ☐ Female ☐ DOB _____ Age _____ S ☐ M ☐
Insurance No.
☐ Medic-Aid
☐ Medicare
☐ Blue Alliance
☐

Patient Taken To:

Next of Kin: Address:

Unit: _____

Type of Call:
Emg. ☐ Semi ☐ Non ☐ No Trans. ☐ Std-By ☐

Crew: 1 Att. _____ ☐ EMT
2 Drv. _____ ☐ EMT
3 _____ ☐ EMT
4 _____ ☐ EMT

Problems Enroute:

☐ Care/Transportation is hereby refused:

Signature _____

Phone: Relation:

TIME RECORD

Call Rec'd.	
Enroute	
At Scene	
From Scene	
At Destination	
Ready for svc	

Hx/Cause

Start Point/Call Location   District

Pulse	BP	Resp.	Cons.	R Pupils L	Time of V/S	Skin	Transport	Communications
			☐ Full ☐ Semi ☐ Un ☐	☐ normal ☐ / ☐ fixed ☐ / ☐ dilated ☐ / ☐ constructed ☐ / ☐ sluggish ☐ / ☐ ☐		☐ normal ☐ pale ☐ moist ☐ blue ☐ hot ☐	☐ face up ☐ face down ☐ semi-fowlers ☐ sitting ☐ on L side ☐ on R side ☐	Hospital notified: ☐ directly ☐ thru dispatch ☐ no ☐
			☐ Full ☐ Semi ☐ Un ☐	☐ normal ☐ / ☐ fixed ☐ / ☐ dilated ☐ / ☐ constructed ☐ / ☐ sluggish ☐ / ☐ ☐		☐ normal ☐ pale ☐ moist ☐ blue ☐ hot	Mileage End: Begin: Total:	Medical Advice Given By: ☐ physician ☐ nurse ☐ none ☐

front   back   **Type**

1 ☐ internal injury
2 ☐ laceration
3 ☐ abrasion
4 ☐ puncture
5 ☐ sprain/strain
6 ☐ fracture/disloc
7 ☐ loss of motion
8 ☐ concussion
9 ☐ pain
10 ☐ burn _____ deg
11 ☐ cardiac problem
12 ☐

Patient's Suspected Problem

☐ Cardiac Arrest
☐ Hemorrhaging
☐ General Illness
☐ Respiratory Distress
☐ Deep Shock
☐ Convulsions/Epilepsy
☐ Vomiting/Nausea
☐ Sprain/Strain
☐ No Apparent Problem

☐ Diabetes
☐ Psychological Problem
☐ Stroke/CVA
☐ Poisoning/Overdose
☐ Impairment similar to that caused by alcohol
☐ Pregnancy
☐ Vaginal Bleeding
☐ Fever _____ ° C ☐ F ☐
☐

Medication Record or Comments

Pre-Hospital Emgy. Care

☐ Airway inserted ─────────
☐ Airway cleared manually
☐ False teeth removed
☐ Suction used
☐ Oxygen: _____ LPM by _____
☐ (Heat) or (Cold) Application
☐ Artificial ventilation ─────────
☐ Bleeding controlled/dressing
☐ CPR—Approx. _____ Min.
☐ Monitored EKG
☐ IV/Medication administered
☐ Defibrillation _____ times @ _____ ws
☐ Spinal immobilization ─────────
☐ Restraints applied
☐ Vomiting induced—time:
    method:
☐ Baby delivered—Time:
    Place:
☐ Limb Immobilization ─────────
☐

☐ oropharengeal
☐ nasal
☐ esophageal
☐

☐ mouth to mouth
☐ bag mask
☐ demand valve
☐

☐ long backboard
☐ short backboard
☐ orthopedic stretcher
☐ cervical collar
☐ sand bags
☐

☐ air
☐ rigid
☐ traction
☐

Prescribing Physician ☐
Patient's Physician ☐

condition that you assume exists—but you cannot medically reach this conclusion.

The "true" degree of a patient's illness or injury cannot ordinarily be determined at the First Responder/EMT level. Often, the ED cannot make the final diagnosis because the condition may be more than an ED can handle.

Although the degree of injury or illness may be apparent to EMS personnel, they should not give a diagnosis. His or her comments should be narrowed to observations, although it is permissible to record "paralysis consistent with cervical fracture."

Review your own medical records. Use this checklist to determine the adequacy and accuracy of their content:

1. Does your record contain all the information needed by others who may rely on your record?

2. Does your record adequately state all your observations about the patient?

3. Can you support or prove all the medical diagnoses you have drawn?

4. Does your record list all treatment given to the patient?

5. Does the treatment fit the observed medical condition of the patient?

6. Is the information complete enough so that you could mentally reconstruct the entire situation and defend your actions at a later date if you needed to?

7. Do your records conform to the detail and information provided by other EMS personnel at your level of care?

With a properly documented record you should be able to answer yes to each question. At this point you have a record that will be a friend, not a foe, in case of later litigation.

Medical records must be completed in a timely manner and in "the ordinary course" of practice. Patient care must come first and take priority. You should never delay patient treatment to complete the record because the loss of time can cause further injury to the patient which is enough of a basis for negligence. Once the patient has received all the aid you can give, complete the record.

Many EMTs complete the record while the patient is in the ambulance undergoing transport. When constant care is needed during transport, the record should be completed as soon as time permits after delivery of the patient to the ED.

It is not proper to complete a record at a later date. A prolonged time delay may cause you to "forget" important observations or treatments given, and you can get confused in recalling the facts relating to one patient or another.

A patient's attorney can challenge the accuracy of your report for these very reasons. He or she may be able to argue that your records were a "later reconstruction" and not records kept in the "ordinary course of practice." Since you can introduce and use records maintained "in the ordinary course of practice" as evidence, timely completion is most important. You cannot use constructed records as evidence.

Some EMTs complete part of the records at the time of service, then complete the record several days later or at the end of the work week or billing cycle. That can be a dangerous practice because the accuracy and legitimacy of the entire record can be thrown into question.

CORRECTING YOUR MEDICAL RECORDS

You will want to make changes or modifications to your medical records regularly. You may want to add information previously omitted, or perhaps you believe the observations about a patient's condition can be stated more accurately. How medical records or an EMT's "run report" should be changed is of considerable legal importance. You must consider that a later change or alteration of an original record can logically be looked at by a patient's attorney and the courts as an attempt to "cover up" information that is damaging to the emergency care personnel.

A report that has obvious erasures or "cross-outs" in it leads to the obvious question: why? What was in the original report that was changed? At the very least it will bring into question the accuracy of the original contents. At worst, a jury may well conclude that faced with a malpractice claim, the EMS defendant intentionally changed or falsified the record. Neither possibility puts the EMS defendant in an enviable position.

Many malpractice attorneys try to get the records under a false excuse and file suit later. The EMS personnel may have forgotten that they gave a copy of the original record to the attorney, or the patient, or even another health provider or agency. After a lawsuit starts, the EMS personnel may be tempted to reconstruct the report to put his or her actions in the best light. Since this tampered or newly constructed report differs from the original, the court will conclude that there is a self-serving motive for the change. If changes or corrections are needed in a report, follow these procedures:

1. Never erase, cross out, or obliterate an original record.

2. You may draw a line through an entry, but it must remain readable.

3. Any change should be stated in a "supplemental report." This lets the reader see both the original report and the changes. The supplemental report should be dated and contain the reasons for the change or corrections.

4. Keeping and the handing out of records should be done by one person in the ambulance service or First Responder unit. This person should be familiar with proper record keeping procedures and make sure the procedures are followed. The individual with this responsibility can also make sure the records are complete and that they are properly released with the date for submission.

5. Should it be suspected that a record is being asked for to start a malpractice suit, the record should be reviewed with the EMS personnel who made the record and the attorney for the firm. It may be that "supplemental information" is required, and at that time it can be completed to make it the most complete, accurate, and defendable report possible.

CONFIDENTIALITY OF RECORDS

Records relating to emergency medical care need the same degree of confidentiality as a patient's other medical records. You cannot give out the contents of a patient's records except under the following conditions:

1. When the patient authorizes a release. The release can be from the patient through a representative such as a guardian, conservator, or administrator or executor if the patient is deceased. Always be sure to get a copy of the patient's representative appointment to satisfy yourself of his or her authority.

   A spouse or other relative does not have the authority to act on behalf of the patient, even if that relative has the authority to consent to treatment for the patient. Whatever the condition of the patient, ignore demands by relatives who seem to be acting on his or her behalf.

   In addition, a patient's attorney has no right to get a release for a patient. Attorneys requesting a patient's records should accompany it with a release authorization signed by the patient. Although there is no legally defined "release form," the authorization should always be in writing, signed by the patient (or his or her court appointed representative), and mark the records asked for, and where they are to be sent.

A sample release may look like the following form:

AUTHORIZATION FOR RELEASE
OF MEDICAL RECORDS

To: XYZ Ambulance Service
     10 Elm Street
     Anytown, U.S.A.

You are hereby authorized to deliver to my attorneys:
White, Weld and Whitaker, 5 Maple Street, Anytown,
U.S.A., all medical records, reports, logs, or information
relating to emergency medical care provided me by your
firm on or about May 10, 1982.

John Jones
_____
Patient

Do not release records based on a verbal request. You cannot
determine the authenticity of the caller, and you lack written
evidence that the release was authorized. Insist on a written
release.

A patient has absolute rights to his or her records. However,
the patient cannot demand the original records because they
are the property rights of the EMS unit. Normally, the patient
will be given copies and can be charged a reasonable fee for
reproduction costs of the records.

2. You can reveal the contents of a patient's records to other health
   care providers without a patient's consent. However, this information must be needed to insure proper treatment for the
   patient in later stages of care. A First Responder can give information to the EMT who in turn will open his or her records
   to the ED personnel. It is this open flow of information between
   emergency care providers that allows for the best patient care.

3. Reasonable information can be given to third-party payment
   plans (such as Blue Cross, Medicaid or Medicare) when it is
   necessary for billing and getting paid. When a patient tells a
   health care provider to bill a third-party, he or she agrees to
   the handing out of all information needed to complete billing.
   Many legal authorities believe that excessive information requires an "invasion of the patient's rights to privacy." However,
   this is of little real concern to EMS providers, as long as they
   give only the information on the billing form.

4. Revealing records under compulsory court order or subpoena would require giving information about the patient's records. EMS personnel often have their records subpoenaed in accident cases, divorce proceedings, or even malpractice cases involving other health providers. The safe course to follow is to have the subpoena checked by the counsel for the EMS unit. If counsel finds it proper he or she will tell you to obey the subpoena. If not, counsel will file a motion to "quash" it.

Contrary to common belief, medical records in most states, although confidential are not "privileged." There is a difference. "Confidentially" means that the provider will not wrongfully reveal or make public information about the patient. "Privilege," on the other hand, makes the record "secretive" and not subject to being revealed through the court process.

Communications and correspondence between an attorney-client, clergyman-parishioner, or husband and wife are generally privileged. An attorney cannot, even under subpoena, reveal confidential information between attorney and client.

In some states this "privilege" will cover a physician and a patient. However, even in these states the privilege does not extend to EMS personnel who are not physicians.

5. State law may demand the reporting of certain incidents without patient approval. These commonly include gunshot wounds, dog bites, certain infectious diseases, and child abuse cases. Where mandatory reporting is required, the EMS personnel will be protected by the existence of the statute. You should familiarize yourself with the incidents that must be reported in your jurisdiction to determine when you must report.

One area of common concern to EMS personnel is their right to reveal patient records to police or other law enforcement agents. Although there are a few cases that suggest revealing information may be legally justified in some instances without patient consent, most hold to the contrary. The safe path to follow is to not voluntarily provide the records, or any information from the records without either the patient's consent or a valid subpoena.

First Responders in a police or fire unit may share both a medical and law enforcement function. Understandably, it may be difficult if not impossible for them to clearly separate their roles. EMT personnel, however, have no real "enforcement" duties and they are lined up with other health care personnel who must hold the patient's records in trust.

Wrongfully revealing medical information can result in liability for "invasion of privacy" or "breach of confidentiality." Unlike a negligence suit, damages may be difficult to prove, but it can be professionally embarrassing and annoying.

Although the question of when you should, and should not, reveal records without patient consent defies certain resolution, the best yardstick to follow is to be liberal in sharing your records with other health practitioners continuing the patient care. To do otherwise may result in negligence by not providing information in a medically prompt manner. On the other hand, do not give others access to the records without a subpoena or written patient consent.

RETAINING THE MEDICAL RECORDS

EMS units not only have a duty to compile adequate records, and hold them confidential, they also have to keep these records for the patient.

How long should patient records be kept? Unfortunately there is no clear answer. However, it should go beyond a point where they could be of any further practical use to the patient. Following the standards of other similar EMS units may provide the key.

Some EMS units asked about this say that they keep the records for 5–6 years. From a patient's viewpoint this may be a long enough time. Of greater concern perhaps is how long to keep the records from the viewpoint of the EMS unit.

Sticking to the policy that the record can be vital to the defense of a malpractice claim, keeping the record should go beyond the time limit in which a malpractice suit can be started. Although the statute of limitations may be 3–4 years in most states, a case may be started many years later if the patient only "recently" discovered the malpractice—or in cases where the patient was a minor.

It is not common, but legal actions have started 10–15 years after service was given. This is one reason many EMS units keep records active for 3–4 years and then place older records in "dead" storage rather than destroy them.

Many other firms put their records on microfilm to avoid storage charges. Regardless of your procedure it is best to hold onto the records. Considering that your records can prevent serious malpractice problems, they deserve the best care and preservation.

TEST YOUR KNOWLEDGE

1. List the parties or bodies who may rely on the completeness and accuracy of your records.

2. Explain how incomplete records can increase your liability in a malpractice suit?

3. How should you handle corrections to your original records?

4. Under what circumstances can you reveal a patient's records?

5. Can you be forced to produce a patient's records with a court subpoena or are the records privileged?

6. Should you reveal a patient's records to police or law enforcement personnel without a warrant or subpoena?

7. For what period of time should you keep patient records?

8. Who owns the original records? Are there any circumstances where you can refuse to provide a patient with a copy of his or her record?

12

METHODS FOR PREVENTING LIABILITY

"An ounce of prevention is worth a pound of cure." This saying applies very well to the subject of malpractice.

It is interesting to note that health care professionals place an increased emphasis on "preventative medicine." At the same time there should be an increased awareness of what can be done in the area of "preventative liability."

In this chapter we will summarize steps you can take to avoid, or to at least reduce, the likelihood of a malpractice case. The second part of this chapter will deal with malpractice insurance. In reality this is an important part of your strategy to get rid of any financial risk resulting from liability.

The first step in any "preventative liability" program is to show a need for awareness. Undoubtedly, this awareness has already been felt in the emergency care field, as seen not only by the defensive attitudes of many EMS personnel, but also by courses on malpractice, articles, reports, and even books such as this one, giving the EMS industry information on the various avenues of liability.

Knowing about malpractice will probably not make a practitioner be free from negligence claims. That will never be the case. Malpractice seldom results from a conscious lack of understanding, but from personal traits and habits, the practitioner's approach to patients, and the practice of his or her profession. Practitioners prone to suits often have work habits that will always place them in the courtroom. Their intellectual awareness of the total malpractice law can never offset poor work habits and hostile patient relationships. This may be summed up by saying that it is more important to be a good health practitioner than it is to be a good lawyer.

Nevertheless, even the most careful practitoner can be the target of a malpractice suit. We are all human and prone to error. However, it is important that all EMS providers know what their professional responsibilities are, and know what circumstances are most likely to create legal difficulty. There are no simple rules to avoid liability, but there are certain "signals" that can caution you to take special care.

Additionally, most malpractice cases result from a set pattern of events that point out potential "trouble spots." Many of these trouble spots involve not only technical error but error in understanding patients and reducing the areas of friction that usually occur between patient and EMS provider. It may be accurate to say that the one ingredient that can best get rid of the prospects for a malpractice suit is common sense.

A TWELVE-POINT CHECKLIST TO REDUCE LIABILITY

Review the following checklist to reduce the chances of a courtroom encounter.

1.   Know the Patient

Some patients are professional plaintiffs. Whether they are motivated to sue everybody for monetary reasons, or because they honestly believe they are always harmed is a matter of independent determination. Physicians obviously have an increased opportunity to evaluate a patient's personality and tendency to sue than EMS personnel who have a limited and brief exposure to a patient in a crisis situation.

Patients who are hostile, argumentative, demanding, or even threaten you with a lawsuit should certainly put you on notice that special care must be taken to calm the patient, and to be consciously aware that treatment should be structured from a legal as well as a medical viewpoint. A safe strategy when dealing with a hostile or threatening patient is to have your treatment reviewed by other EMS personnel. You may not be able to avoid the litigation-prone patient, but you can take the extra steps to make sure that the patient has no basis for a suit.

2.   Don't Promise Optimistic Results

One of the most serious errors that can be made by EMS personnel is to try to reduce a patient's concern by promising optimistic results.

An EMT may comfort a patient with well-intentioned words that "you will be okay" or "it's nothing serious," only to have the patient find out that he or she does have a serious medical problem. At that point the patient may begin to question the judgment of the EMT, or even wonder whether his or her condition was the result of negligent treatment. To a degree it is only logical that if a practitioner promises or even suggests a certain end result, the patient will be rightfully disappointed with anything less. EMS personnel are seldom in a position to diagnose a patient. Although the diagnosis may be well-intentioned, it is beyond the scope of emergency care and can create resentment and encourage a lawsuit.

3.   Know Your Level of Competence

Do not perform procedures you may not be equipped or competent enough to handle. Many EMS personnel have distorted views of what is expected of them and they perform procedures or treatment that is beyond the scope of their field, or should be reserved for the ED.

Part of this problem is undoubtedly due to the emergence of emergency care as a specialty and the separation of its various practitioners. However, an EMT should not needlessly perform treatment normally done by paramedics, and no emergency care provider should attempt treatment not needed before delivery to the hospital.

Ambulance services and emergency units have the corresponding duty to appoint emergency services to staff members that have the proven skill and competency to perform the services expected on the call.

4.   Obtain Other Opinions

When a course of action is questionable, EMS personnel should get the opinion of other EMS personnel at the scene. Your judgment on the matter can be reinforced through support from co-workers. Not only can this technique avoid serious error, but it also tends to have a marked effect if a malpractice suit is started. A jury may believe that one EMS provider may make an error in judgment, but the chance of two providers being in error defies probability.

5.   Avoid Unusual Treatment

There are rapid technological and procedural changes being made in emergency care. However, a practitioner who is too advanced or "experimental" in his or her approach may be as liable as the practitioner who is backwards and does not stay ahead of what is going on in his or her field.

Emergency care practitioners are evaluated against the existing standards of other emergency care practitioners. Extremes in either direction are risky. Do not try new techniques or treatment unless these procedures have been generally adopted by others. Being progressive to the point of being "far ahead of the pack" may be professionally rewarding but still create needless legal exposure.

6.   Develop Good Patient Relationships

Another frequently mentioned reason for many malpractice cases is that the patient simply disliked the practitioner. Even in emergency care, where contact between you and the patient is short, you may negatively communicate with the patient or have a "personality clash."

It is difficult to sue someone you like. If you know how to handle patients, the likelihood of a malpractice suit is greatly decreased. Many patients realize that a practitioner may have provided negligent treatment and still refused to sue because they liked the practitioner.

Developing good human relations is partially a matter of personality and to that degree it cannot be taught. The best we can do is outline the characteristics patients resent the most when dealing with emergency care personnel. These characteristics include:

- a real or imagined lack of concern about the patient.
- needless hostility or an arrogant attitude toward the patient.
- a failure to communicate adequately.
- not enough attention given to the patient.

Of all the health care providers, EMS personnel need to have the most sensitivity toward the human relationship aspects of patient care. They are dealing in a crisis situation with emotionally wrought patients. Sympathy and psychology are as important as technical skills. Remember, what you say, and how you say it, can prevent a "would-be" lawsuit.

7.   Maintain Good Records

Adequate records not only indicate an orderly approach to emergency care, but they can also be a major weapon in the defense of a malpractice case. Attorneys usually investigate a case before they start a suit. Adequate records can often explain an unfavorable result that otherwise may be thought to result from negligence. Poor record keeping, even if the records themselves are not relevant to the case, can lead the jury to conclude that the practitioner is "sloppy," and the "carry-over" effect can influence their decision about the issues in point.

8.   Do Not Press A Hostile Patient For Payment

There are many patients who will not pay a practitioner because they are unhappy with the treatment. Ambulance services may serve patients who used their dissatisfaction as a basis for non-payment. In some cases an ambulance service will sue for payment only to have the patient counterclaim with a malpractice claim. Faced with a hostile patient who refuses to pay, it is usually wise not to press for payment.

9.   Do Not Admit Your Mistakes

You will eventually commit errors in judgment or do something wrong. The error may be minor and meaningless. Do not compound the problem by telling the patient or admitting it. Admitting an error or negligence can be used as evidence in court. This admission will point you out as a defendant if the patient is not satisfied with his or her treatment.

Be equally careful about what you say to other EMS personnel in the presence of even a comatose patient. Often a patient will appear unconscious and still be aware of what is being said. Statements made to other EMS personnel can create legal problems. You have no assurance that what you said will be held confidential, or that it will not be used against you in the result of a malpractice suit.

If you do acknowledge an error, take immediate steps to correct or minimize it, and do not admit it to anyone except your supervisor if it is an important error.

10.   Remain Competent

You are expected to practice with the same degree of skill and knowledge demonstrated by your colleagues. This places the obligation on you to keep up with new developments in emergency care. Attending continuing education seminars, subscribing to professional journals and newsletters, and reviewing new books in the field can keep you current and improve your skill. Original licensure or certification is no assurance that you have the needed qualifications years later. You have the self-imposed obligation to make certain you remain competent.

11.   Practice In Compliance With All Laws

Emergency care practitioners are subject to laws, regulations, accreditation standards, and recommendations and ethical codes from associations. These guidelines become the operative and accepted methods for practice.

You can decrease the chances of liability by becoming totally familiar with all the laws of emergency care passed in your state. Considering the diversity of state laws, no one book can cover all the laws except in a general way. You have the obligation to check your state law and follow it. Ignorance of the law is not only a worthless excuse, but it can cause major legal problems.

12.   Do What's Best For the Patient

The one difficulty in providing advice in a book such as this, or any other book, is that the information tends to create a set of "do's" and "don'ts." No book can really address every possible situation, and no two cases are identical. What this book or any other book recommends, and even what you may have learned in school or a training program, is at best only a generalization.

Do not be bound by the written word. There will be many cases where you will have to do the unusual or break from traditional approaches to protect the patient.

If you do what is best for the patient's welfare—and do it properly with all the skill and concern that you can provide—you will have no reason to worry about a lawsuit. It all comes back to that one essential ingredient that all EMS personnel must have—common sense.

MALPRACTICE INSURANCE

Any discussion on preventing or reducing liability must include a discussion about insurance. Having malpractice insurance does not reduce liability because a judgment can still be entered against you. However, it does shift the financial risk because the insurance underwriter is obligated to defend the case and pay the claim to the degree of policy coverage.

Malpractice insurance has been a problem for health providers in the past 10–15 years. Many insurance companies have dropped out of the malpractice coverage field due to escalating claims. Others have greatly increased their premiums to a level that few providers can afford. Other companies are highly selective in deciding who they will insure, offering coverage only to providers with no previous malpractice suits.

EMTs and paramedics have met resistance from insurance companies. Insurance companies point to the increased involvement of EMTs in malpractice cases. Municipally employed First Responders also have difficulty finding enthusiastic insurers because insurance companies attach little importance to the protection given by Good Samaritan laws.

Many EMS personnel take the position that they do not need malpractice coverage. In some cases they may be correct because they may have enough protection provided by employer coverage or operate with almost total immunity under the Good Samaritan laws. Others argue that they have little to lose even if they are sued. Let's consider each of these arguments in greater detail.

1.   Employer Provided Coverage

EMTs assume that the ambulance service employing them carries enough malpractice insurance, and in most instances that assumption is correct.

The practical problem of relying on an employer's coverage is that the insurance company may not be obligated to defend on behalf of the employee or pay a judgment brought against the employee. The latter consideration is perhaps not of practical importance because the employer will be liable for the negligent actions of the employee. Therefore, a judgment against the employee will logically result in the same judgment against the employer. Since the employer's judgment will be satisfied by the insurance company, the payment on behalf of the employer will likewise satisfy the claim against the employee.

EMS personnel relying on employer coverage still run considerable risk. For example:

- How does an employee pay the costs of defending himself if the insurance company refuses to?

- What protection does an employer have if the insurance company takes the position that the employer is not liable for the acts of the employee occurring beyond the scope of his or her employment?

- How can the employee be protected by the employer's insurance if the employer's insurance was cancelled?

- What if the employer does not carry enough insurance, leaving the employee unprotected against any claim for a large amount?

It can happen that an employee ignores the problem of insurance coverage only to find that the employee's coverage is useless to them once a case is filed.

My recommendations to all EMS personnel relying on employer coverage is to follow these procedures:

1. Review the policy and satisfy yourself that the insurance un-

derwriter is obligated to defend not only the employer but the
employee as well.

2. Consider the coverage. In an era of high malpractice awards a
judgment of $500,000–$1,000,000 is no longer rare. Be sure the
coverage is at least $500,000 per patient incident.

3. Consider the financial stability of the employer. Many ambulance services facing financial problems will either reduce their
coverage to save on premiums or worse, let the coverage be
cancelled due to non-payment of premiums. Another possibility is that the ambulance service may file for bankruptcy or
reorganization during the malpractice suit trial. This defense
can be used by the insurance company to refuse payment. Your
goal is to satisfy yourself that the coverage you are relying on
will remain in force and not be cancelled due to your employer's
poor financial condition.

First Responders and paramedics employed by municipalities have
an additional problem. If the municipality can raise the defense of
governmental immunity to avoid liability, that defense may negate
the obligation of the insurance company to pay. Unless the policy
expressly provides that the insurance company will defend and indemnify the employee, the insurance may be of no practical benefit
to you.

2.   Assessing the Defenses Available to EMS Personnel

Many EMS personnel believe that they have little or no exposure to
liability due to the Good Samaritan laws. If you review Chapter 5,
you will see that the Good Samaritan statutes may offer you less
protection than you think. Even if the laws do provide a possibility
for immunity, a patient may decide to challenge how the statute was
applied, forcing you to spend lots of money to defend yourself or go
bankrupt.

Experience in past cases shows that many patients are not discouraged by the Good Samaritan laws, especially when the defendant
is an EMS provider instead of a lay person. For these reasons, I do
not consider Good Samaritan laws an acceptable substitute for adequate insurance coverage.

3.   The Risks of Having No Insurance Coverage

Since many EMS personnel are essentially wage earners, they may
decide to "go bare" and not get insurance based on the theory that

they have few personal assets to lose even if they are sued, so why go to the expense of paying for insurance? Poverty is a big drawback to a plaintiff because the theory that you cannot "get blood from a stone" is true.

EMS personnel may still have assets that may not be worth a lot, but they may still be important. A home, motor vehicles, or even an inheritance can be threatened by a lawsuit. Transferring these assets to a "straw" upon the commencement of a lawsuit is not practical because the plaintiff can easily attack the transfer as being fraudulent. There are EMS personnel who report they have absolutely no personnel assets to risk. For these individuals, a malpractice suit can easily be dismissed by filing bankruptcy. This raises the practical question of whether the premium payments are worth the price of filing for personal bankruptcy. Of course, there is no easy answer because each person has to determine his or her own relative values.

Ambulance services often ask the same question. Many private services are incorporated and have few assets to lose or they have their assets secured to a bank or other lender giving the plaintiff no practical means. In some cases an ambulance service will lease its ambulances and have nothing in assets except for accounts receivable.

An ambulance service that is essentially "judgment proof" may decide to save on large annual premiums by waiving malpractice insurance. The only reasons why "judgment proof" ambulance services may carry insurance is because 1) their employees demand the protection, or 2) their contracts with municipalities may require insurance.

This does not mean that "judgment proof" ambulance services should not carry insurance. They may have to defend countless "nuisance" suits of questionable liability. The premiums for insurance may be much less than the costs to defend against these claims. As with all business decisions, the ambulance service will have to weigh the benefits against the costs.

THE STRUCTURE OF A MALPRACTICE POLICY

Malpractice coverage is no different from any other type of insurance coverage. The insured party pays a premium and in return the insurance company agrees to defend and compensate the insured subject to the conditions of the policy. The insurance policy is a contractual obligation that states the duties and obligations of both the insured party and the insurance company.

Consider the elements of malpractice policy shown below.

1.   Premiums

How much the insurance coverage will cost depends on many variables:

- EMT's usually have to pay more than municipally employed First Responders because they have a higher claim rate.
- Geographic location. The incidence of claims depends on geography. EMS personnel in the West and metropolitan centers have the highest chances of facing claims.
- Prior claims. Some insurance carriers add an extra risk premium for EMS personnel who have had prior claims made against them.
- Coverage. This is the major factor in deciding on premiums because it defines the risk of the insurance company. Obviously it will cost less to insure for $100,000 than $500,000, but that does not mean the $500,000 coverage will be five times as expensive. There is a much greater probability that the insurer may face a $100,000 claim than a $500,000. Therefore, higher coverage will cost more but cost appreciably less proportionately as the coverage expands. Other factors that decide premiums include the scope of coverage, and whether the insured party will pay part of the claim under a co-deductible clause.

Aside from modifying the coverage, EMS may find that they can greatly reduce premiums by subscribing for insurance on a "group rate" or through plans sponsored by professional associations. This should be investigated before you buy insurance on your own.

2.   Scope of Coverage

The policy will define the type of errors and negligence that are covered. Ordinarily the policy will be broad enough to cover all types of negligence resulting from your work. However, you should review your policy if the nature of your position changes. For example, coverage to a First Responder may not grant the responder coverage if he or she later becomes an EMT.

Insurance does not cover all sources of liability. In some cases the exclusions are stated within the policy and in other cases the exclusions exist by common law. Acts that you may not be insured against—exclusions—include:

- assault and battery
- defamation

- invasion of privacy
- revealing confidential information
- false imprisonment
- intentional wrongdoing
- acts that involve a violation of a law or regulation

Looking at standard malpractice coverage from the opposite viewpoint of what is covered, you may find that insurance will only protect you against non-intentional errors and negligence when no violation of a law exists. Unfortunately, these exclusions can be important to EMS personnel because it is possible that liability may result from an excluded act.

Assault and battery can result from treating a patient without proper consent. Invasion of privacy or defamation can result when a patient's records are revealed. False imprisonment exists when an EMT may transport a patient against the patient's will. Some insurance companies will insure against these risks and serious thought should be given to obtaining coverage for these risks because they do occur in emergency care.

3.   Term of Coverage

Some policies cover claims regardless of when the suit is filed. Others structure their policy to cover claims actually made within the year even though the negligent act occurred several years earlier. This is known as a "claims made" policy. It helps the insurance company because they can determine the amount of their potential liability at the close of the insurance year since they are not responsible for claims filed later, even though the negligent act took place during the year of coverage.

Either type of coverage is acceptable to EMS providers. However, EMS providers should buy insurance that consistently provides coverage. A policy that covers claims filed in the year of coverage forces the EMS provider to renew the policy to maintain the coverage if a suit occurs at a later date.

4.   Deductibles

We mentioned "co-deductible" provisions earlier in this chapter. Here is how they work. If a policy has a deductible of $2,500, then the insurance company would be obligated to pay an award in excess of that amount because the insured party would have to pay the first $2,500 under the claim.

Frequently the insurance company will offer the insured the right to select the amount of the deductible. As the deductible increases the premium is reduced since a larger part of the risk is being paid by the insured.

In selecting a deductible amount it should be consistent with your ability to pay. It makes no sense to agree to a $5,000 deductible unless you are prepared to pay it should a claim occur.

5.   Duties of the Insurance Company

The insurance company has to defend against the claim even if the claim exceeds the amount of coverage. In addition, the insurance company must pay any award up to the amount of the policy limit (less any deductibles).

There are situations where the rights of the insured conflict with an insurance company. For example, an EMT may have a $100,000 policy. What if the insurance company wants to settle for $50,000 but the EMT opposes this and a later judgment is entered for $75,000? Many malpractice policies need the approval of the insured party before settlement can be made as the settlement may create a poor professional reputation. This provision is common where physicians are insured. However, it is not frequently used when EMS personnel are insured. When they are in effect, most policies state that the insurance company will not be liable for an amount in excess of what the case could have been settled for if the insured party refuses settlement. When no such "right to accept settlement" agreement exists, an insurance company has the right to settle and pay the claim, even over the objection of the insured party.

On the other hand, an EMT with a $100,000 policy may be sued for $200,000. Also, a plaintiff may offer to settle within the policy limits only to have the insurance company refuse the offer.

An insurance company has the obligation to act reasonably and in "good faith" to protect its insured party. If an offer of settlement is negligently declined causing excess liability to the insured, the insured has the right to force the insurance company to pay the "excess," even beyond the policy limit.

6.   Duties of the Insured

You have certain roles under the policy. Your main duty is to co-operate fully with the insurance company to defend the claim. This requires you to fully communicate and reveal all relevant information to counsel for the insurance company; to go to hearings and answer other forms of discovery; and to take part in and testify at the time of trial. Where an insured party does not cooperate the insurance company may decline coverage under the policy.

Generally you are not obligated to tell your insurance company about a possible claim until you are actually sued. However, it is good policy to involve your insurance company whenever there is a reasonable basis to believe you will be sued. Often early intervention by the insurance company will prevent the revealment of damaging evidence, or a reduced settlement may be made directly with the patient before the start of a lawsuit.

When the policy is issued on a "claims made" basis (making the insurance company pay all claims filed that year, regardless of when they happened), you will be required to reveal any incidents that you believe may develop into a lawsuit. This is necessary for the insurance company to determine the risk before they agree to insure you. A false statement can disqualify coverage. However, the courts do not generally let the insurance companies use this defense unless there is a clear showing that the insured had a reasonable expectation of a lawsuit that was not disclosed.

At best, this chapter only gave you a broad overview of malpractice insurance. It is a highly complex and technical contract. For this reason your policy should be reviewed either by legal counsel or an agent who knows your insurance needs. With a well-designed malpractice policy, EMS personnel will be free of the financial angles of their negligent acts. They may begin to shed the "defensive" ways in which emergency care is often given. This will certainly be to the benefit of the patient and EMS providers alike because effective medical care rather than legal implications should rule the emergency care setting.

TEST YOUR KNOWLEDGE

1. Why should you not give a patient a good diagnosis on his or her condition?

2. If you admit to a negligent act may it be used against you later in a malpractice suit?

3. What are the practical problems in relying on employer provided malpractice insurance?

4. What factors influence the cost of malpractice insurance?

5. What is meant by a "deductible clause" in a malpractice policy?

6. List the types of wrongful acts that a standard malpractice policy may not insure against.

ANSWERS TO THE MOST COMMON QUESTIONS ON LAW IN EMERGENCY CARE

1. Q. Can EMS personnel avoid liability by having a patient sign a release in advance of treatment?
   A. No. All states consider pretreatment releases as being against public policy and without legal effect. This should not be confused with a release where a patient refuses treatment or transport that would generally be binding if the patient had the mental capacity to refuse treatment.

2. Q. **How should an EMT handle a situation where a patient is comatose and a spouse or relative is hysterical and refuses to let the EMT treat or transport the patient?**
   A. This is a frequent problem. Non-consent by a spouse can legally restrict an EMT. However, for the spouse to issue a valid consent or non-consent, she must have enough mental competency.

      If the patient needs immediate care, the spouse should be told, and if she still refuses, she should sign a release. In many cases the spouse will agree to transport or treatment if she can remain with the husband during transport and this should be offered. Certainly, every effort should be made to obtain a spouse's consent where the refusal to consent is not rational.

3. Q. **Under what circumstances can EMS personnel be held criminally liable for negligently causing the death of a patient?**
   A. For negligently-caused death to be criminal the acts would have to be "wanton, willful, and reckless conduct." This means that the EMS provider performed treatment totally disregarding the welfare or safety of the patient. This does not mean actual intent, but rather an extreme case of negligent conduct. It is only at this point when a case for manslaughter exists. Any lesser degree of negligence is only civil in nature.

4. Q. **Is a hospital under an obligation to admit an emergency case?**

A. The law is not clear on this point. However, most cases state that the obligation to admit exists if:

a. The hospital holds itself out as routinely accepting emergency cases, or

b. The hospital is owned or controlled by a government agency that has the duty to give emergency care to the public.

A hospital can refuse treatment for acceptable reasons, including not being able to give the type care needed by the patient or lack of space. However, they should give the necessary treatment within their power until transfer to another facility can be arranged.

5. Q. **Can an EMT's records be used as evidence in a malpractice case?**

A. Yes, providing the records were kept in the ordinary or usual routine. This forces the duty on EMTs to properly maintain records with the understanding that they may someday be examined by a court.

6. Q. **What should an ambulance service do if a third party requests copies of a patient's records?**

A. They should decline unless they have the prior written approval of the patient. The only exception to this would be where the records are asked for under a valid subpoena, or are used by the ED to coordinate emergency care.

7. Q. **Can a First Responder be held liable for negligence if he or she gives the aid without expecting payment?**

A. Possibly. Payment or providing the service for a fee is not needed to file a negligence case. A non-paid volunteer can be liable. The Good Samaritan laws will, however, give greater protection to the non-paid volunteer as the statutes usually leave out practitioners providing the service for a fee.

8. Q. **Do police have the right to prevent an EMT from providing necessary treatment or transport?**

A. Yes. Police can totally control the emergency scene, including arrangements for the patient. The EMT should tell the police why treatment is necessary, record the police intervention, and should remain in attendance until the patient is removed by the police. Often police will let the EMT give aid or transport after a police investigation is completed. For this reason an EMT should not leave the scene while there is still a possibility he or she can help. An EMT should never resist or interfere with the order of the police.

9. Q. **Can police order an EMT to give a specific treatment or participate in the administration of a breathalyzer or blood-alcohol test?**

A. No. The police can prevent treatment but they do not have the right to affirmatively order an EMT to act. What treatment an EMT provides should be determined by the EMT. EMTs should not participate in the police efforts to determine intoxication as this can create liability for the EMT.

10. Q. **To what degree can a patient's hospital choice override the EMT hospital?**

A. When there is no potential danger to the patient in transporting him or her to the hospital of his or her choice, the patient's decision should be followed. When a patient's hospital choice would add to the period of transport, to the detriment of the patient, the nearer hospital should be used. The patient can arrange for transfer after emergency care is provided.

11. Q. **Can an EMT treat a patient in need of emergency care if the person is mentally competent but refuses help?**

A. No. A mentally competent person has the right to decide whether or not to consent to emergency treatment. Any attempt to treat or transport the patient without his or her permission can make you liable for assault, battery, and false imprisonment. About all you can do in this situation is to have the patient sign a release form and urge the patient to get care. If the patient is mentally incompetent, (intoxicated, comatose, or emotionally disturbed) you can give aid without consent if the treatment is necessary to preserve the health or life of the patient.

12. Q. **If a First Responder working for a municipality negligently treats a patient, can he or she be held liable, or will he or she be protected by governmental immunity?**

A. Governmental immunity is a defense for the governmental employer. It cannot be used by an employee of the municipality. A First Responder, unlike a privately employed EMT, may however have a defense to liability under the Good Samaritan statute.

13. Q. **Can a private ambulance service refuse assistance on the basis of race, or must they accept all patients.**

A. Private ambulance services can refuse to contract with a patient. However, they cannot discriminate due to race, religion, national origin, or sex, if the service receives direct or indirect funding from the government. Participation under Medicaid or Medicare programs may be enough to require the ambulance service to follow both Federal and State equal rights and non-discrimination statutes.

14. Q.   **Is it legal for an ambulance service to refuse Medicaid patients?**

    A.   In the absence of a municipal contract or state regulation requiring services to publicly aided patients, an ambulance service can refuse a Medicaid patient if the ambulance service did not start treatment, or the patient did not bring on a delay in treatment due to the refusal. This would force the duty on the ambulance service to determine whether the patient is on Medicaid when the call for service is received, and to decline service at that time. You can be liable for negligence if the patient expects treatment and transport and you decline it at the scene of the accident.

15. Q.   **If a paramedic receives instructions from an ED through telemetry, can he or she be held liable if the treatment proves negligent?**

    A.   This will depend on the facts. If the negligence was due to a misdiagnosis or an error in judgment by the ED, the paramedic will generally not be liable if he or she properly communicated symptoms and life signs, and followed the instructions properly. One exception to this rule is where the paramedic knew or should have known that the instructions were improper.

16. Q.   **Can an EMT physically hold down a suicide patient without his or her consent?**

    A.   The EMT not only can but must. A suicide patient clearly does not have the mental competency to give or withhold consent. Therefore, the EMT must take all reasonable steps to protect the patient from further self-inflicted injury.

17. Q.   **If an EMT notices a patient trying to get rid of contraband drugs, can the EMT forcibly take the drugs from the patient?**

    A.   No. This is beyond the range of emergency medical care and could subject the EMT to a suit for assault and battery, as well as personal harm. It is best to only observe the situation and report it to the police. Police First Responders, however, may have the right to seize the evidence as it would be helpful to their role of enforcement.

18. Q.   **If a negligent treatment causes no physical damage or injury, can a patient recover for any alleged mental trauma?**

    A.   Mental trauma without physical injury is no cause for suit in most states. The reason for this is that mental trauma cannot readily be verified and it could be a false claim. In recent years some states have awarded damages for mental trauma or anguish and this trend is likely to continue. Wrongful acts, such as assault, battery, false imprisonment, and defamation may create liability for mental anguish since the wrongful act was done on purpose.

19. Q. **Can an ambulance service that is responsible for liability due to the negligence of an employee EMT seek reimbursement from the EMT?**

A. Technically, the employer can sue the employee for repayment. Such an action is rare as employees seldom have the financial capability to repay the employer.

20. Q. **Would a trucking company be liable for negligent treatment provided by one of their employees who stopped to give aid to an injured motorist?**

A. An employer will be liable (together with the employee) if the negligent act happened within the scope of the employment. An act is within the "scope of employment" if the act is close enough to what the employee was hired to do or was reasonably close to his or her job. If the employee, out of habit, stopped to give aid and this was known and approved by the employer, it logically would be an act for which the employer would share responsibility. However, cases such as this usually end up as an issue for the jury to decide.

21. Q. **Can an ED physician be held liable for the acts of a paramedic where the paramedic performed the improper treatment within the ED?**

A. Possibly. If the paramedic was under the direct supervision and control of the physician, the physician would be liable under the "borrowed servant" doctrine. Of course, the patient may also claim liability against the physician on the basis that he or she was negligent by not properly supervising the paramedic. EMS personnel can have automatic liability for the negligent acts of someone else's employee when the employee is under their direct control.

22. Q. **Can a minor who is 16–17 years of age consent to medical treatment or is it necessary to get parental consent?**

A. This would depend on whether the minor needed emergency treatment or the provisions of your state law. Consent is not needed when a minor patient needs immediate emergency treatment. When immediate treatment is not needed, a minor may be able to grant lawful consent when he is independent of his parents. This means that the child is living apart from the parents and the parents no longer provide or are in a position to control the child.

Most states have independent child provisions letting the minor act for himself, although the minimum age requirement is usually 16.

23. Q. **Under what circumstances can a patient request termination of transport and leave an ambulance?**

    A. A patient can always withdraw consent to treatment or transport, and if the patient has the mental capacity to do so it should be honored. As with all "non-consent" situations, the EMT should give enough warnings and cautions and try to get a patient release.

24. Q. **If a patient does not understand English, is it necessary to get the services of a translator who can communicate in the patient's native tongue before treatment can begin?**

    A. Not in an emergency situation. No case law forces this duty on EMS personnel. In fact, the delay in getting a translator may create further injury and cause a negligence claim. EMS personnel should through gestures make every effort to make the patient understand the nature of the intended treatment. In a hospital setting, the need for translation may exist to legally obtain consent as there may be enough time for such activity.

25. Q. **If a patient dies during transport, should the EMT notify the relatives?**

    A. No. The EMT has no legal authority to pronounce death and the EMT should continue all possible life support measures. It is the responsibility of the ED physician to determine a DOA case and to tell relatives. Even where the EMT is certain death occurred and a direct inquiry is made by a relative, the EMT should carefully refer the patient to the ED.

26. Q. **Can a First Responder or EMT be liable if a patient causes injury to a bystander?**

    A. Yes, if they knew or had reasonable cause to believe the patient could be a possible danger to bystanders and had a chance to prevent the patient from acting and did not take timely action. Certainly this danger exists when handling intoxicated, suicidal, or emotionally disturbed patients. In such cases, immediate action should be taken to remove bystanders from the scene and hold down the patient.

27. Q. **If an EMT is called on a child abuse case, can the EMT remove or transport the child without parental consent?**

    A.   No, parental consent is required. However, the EMT should remain to protect the child until the police arrive.

28. Q. **When does the responsibility of the EMT begin and end?**

    A.   It begins upon arrival at the scene when responsibility is transferred from the First Responder, and continues until the patient is accepted by and under the actual care of the hospital ED.

29. Q. **Are First Responders held to the standard of care (skill and competence) of lay persons or are they required to perform with a higher degree of care?**

    A.   First Responders have a higher standard expected of them due to their training and certification. They are expected to know more—and do more than what can be expected from the general public.

30. Q. **Can an ambulance service be liable if it fails to respond to an emergency call within a reasonable time?**

    A.   It can be liable if the ambulance does not arrive within a response time normally anticipated or expected by industry standards, unless the delay was caused by circumstances beyond the control of the ambulance service. Where response cannot be timely made, the dispatcher should either refuse service or arrange for alternate service.

31. Q. **Under what circumstances can an ambulance service be held liable when it operates a "one-man" ambulance service?**

    A.   An ambulance service has the duty to provide enough staffing to go with the type of treatment needed or critical condition of the patient.

       When an ambulance service is told the nature of the problem, it must send personnel, enough both in terms of number and qualification, needed to give proper patient care. Leaving a critically injured or ill patient alone during transport can create liability if the patient suffers further injury that could have been avoided through on-going treatment and supervision.

32. Q. **Can an EMT make ED personnel accompany a patient during interhospital transfer?**

    A.   This condition can be forced as a condition of transfer, and is highly recommended if the patient is likely to need the intensive care that can best be provided by ED staff rather than EMTs.

33. Q. **What is the liability of an ambulance service that "screens" a call and wrongfully decides emergency care is not required?**

A. This depends on whether a pre-existing duty to respond exists between the ambulance service and the patient. If the ambulance service is under a municipal contract, or is the only service reasonably available in that location, the duty to respond is much greater.

Whether the ambulance service will be held liable depends on the adequacy of the screening technique by the dispatcher, and the reasonableness of his or her decision once all the needed information was received. It may be economically and logistically impossible to "roll on every call." However, the benefit of the doubt certainly should lean toward the patient.

34. Q. **Does an EMT have the obligation to report a rape situation to the police?**

A. Most reporting requirements place the duty on the ED rather than on the EMT. However, local law should be consulted to determine the exact reporting requirements not only for rape, but also for gunshot wounds, animal bites, evidence of a felony, suicide, and contagious diseases. The EMT has the obligation to give the ED all information necessary for the ED to make a full report.

35. Q. **What type of negligence is most common in lawsuits against EMTs?**

A. Statistically, an EMT faces the greatest risk when treating patients with neck and head injury. This type of case has the highest claim incidence. For this reason, EMT's should approach a patient with possible neck and head injury (spinal or cervical injury) with the utmost care to prevent further trauma.

36. Q. **Can an EMT pass duties on to a First Responder, members of a rescue squad, or bystanders?**

A. Passing on duties is only proper if absolutely needed due to a shortage of EMT personnel in a disaster situation. If the EMT has enough opportunity to give the necessary care, he or she could be liable for any negligent act caused by a person working under his or her supervision.

37. Q. **Is it legal to use a tape recorder to record conversations and statements made in an ambulance?**

A. A tape recorder is an excellent idea because it can document what was, and was not, said and can provide essential evidence in any lawsuit, or to record the dying declarations of a patient. Prior to recording, the patient should be told of the tape recorder and agree to its use. Any recording should be held confidential to the same degree as medical records.

38. Q. **Can relatives of a patient who is obviously dead prevent the EMT from moving the patient to a hospital before arrival of a physician?**

A. This is one case where common sense should override strict legal theory. In practice, a patient should be transported and given life support services unless external signs (burns, decapitation, and so on) clearly show that the patient is dead. If there is any remote chance of restoring life, transport should be made or at least attempted. When relatives refuse consent, the proper alternate procedure would be to give life support treatment until an emergency physician arrives.

39. Q. **Is a patient entitled to the original EMT records?**

A. No. The original records are the property of the ambulance service. The patient is entitled to a copy. However, the patient can be charged photocopy and clerical handling expenses.

40. Q. **Is it possible for an EMT/paramedic (advanced EMT) to be prosecuted for performing treatment usually reserved for physicians?**

A. The scope of a paramedic's services is increasingly being defined by new state laws. Most states already have statutes that expressly allow for mobile intensive care units, and authorize paramedics to use advanced life saving techniques. Some procedures need communicated authorization by physicians. Other procedures may be done only by decision of the paramedic.

Paramedics should fully know their state laws that govern their activities. This is the only way to avoid civil or criminal liability.

41. Q. **Can an EMT or paramedic be liable if they fail to communicate patient symptoms and life signs to an ED?**

A. Yes. Constant communication of vital signs and change in condition is necessary for the EMT/paramedic to receive instruction and to adequately prepare the ED for the patient. It is much safer to give the ED more, rather than less, information.

42. Q. **Can an EMT's or paramedic's license be revoked without a hearing?**

A. No. An occupational license is a "property right" and can only be revoked under due process of law. This gives the EMT/paramedic full opportunity to challenge the charges, be represented by counsel, question witnesses, and defend under the same procedural rules as in a court.

The grounds for taking away a license are stated within the specific licensing statutes, but generally include any violation of law or regulation within the profession, such as unfitness due to intoxication or drug dependency; and conviction of a felony.

43. Q. **Can an EMT be held liable if ED personnel remove immobilization equipment from a patient before checking the EMT's records for possible injury?**

A. The EMT has the duty to forewarn and advise the ED of a patient's possible condition before adverse treatment is started. On the other hand, the ED has the duty to get the EMT records, consult, and check the patient's condition. Improper communication between the EMT and the ED can create liability for both.

44. Q. **If a patient refuses treatment or fails to cooperate, causing further harm, would this be contributory negligence on the part of the patient?**

A. It would be if the patient did not act as a reasonably careful person to protect his or her own welfare. The case would certainly be strengthened if the EMT or paramedic told the patient that the patient's behavior could cause the patient further injury. A second defense would be that the patient voluntarily refused consent which ends the responsibility of the EMT if the patient had the capacity to refuse.

45. Q. **What role does an ambulance service's policy and procedures manual play in a malpractice case?**

A. The policy and procedures (or operations) manual can define accepted standards and procedures to be followed by its EMTs. When an EMT does not follow the instructions or procedures in the manual a jury can consider this evidence of negligence because the manual establishes a "standard of care," recognized internally within the company.

This does not suggest that violating an operations manual necessarily will be final evidence of negligence. An EMT may have a justifiable reason for not following the guidelines if the circumstances required it, and in certain cases sticking to the written policy would be negligent.

Ambulance services maintaining operations manuals

should draft the manual to give their EMTs the most flexible guidelines possible. Restrictive guidelines can place
the EMT in a questionable position if he or she decides
that alternate treatment was needed. Protect your EMTs by
creating flexible guidelines rather than rigid rules.

46. Q. **Are there specific laws beyond the general Good Samaritan statutes that provide freedom from suit especially for
lay persons who administer CPR?**

A. Certain states have passed protective statutes giving freedom from suit to persons who give CPR. Most of these
statutes require the person to be certified in CPR by the
American Red Cross or American Heart Association, and
also say that the service must be performed without expecting payment. As with most Good Samaritan statutes,
CPR immunity laws generally do not provide protection
against gross misconduct or wanton, willful or reckless
conduct.

Lay persons and First Responders with CPR training
should review their state laws to determine what special
protection they may have.

47. Q. **Is a senile geriatric patient considered incompetent to consent or to withhold consent to emergency care?**

A. Senility can be one form of mental incapacity. However,
the degree of senility would have to be determined.

The test for mental capacity follows a subjective test.
You must consider whether the patient (1) understands the
nature or severity of his or her illness or injury,
(2) understands the proposed treatment, (3) can appreciate
the need for the treatment, and (4) realizes the risks of
refusing treatment or transport.

This can only be determined by adequately explaining
the situation to the patient and judging the clearness of his
or her response. The fact that a patient may be slow to
respond does not mean he or she does not understand.

As with all consent cases, questionable cases should be
decided in favor of extending treatment.

48. Q. **Does an ambulance service have to provide transport to
a patient who does not need emergency care?**

A. Not generally. Even if an EMT responds to a call, he or she
can refuse transport if the patient can arrange for alternate
or later transport without further danger to himself.

Of course, every effort should be made by the EMT to
determine that the patient does not need emergency care
because the EMT would be liable if the patient did require

immediate treatment and transport was wrongfully refused. For this reason all but the most obvious cases of non-
emergency should receive the requested transport. This is
especially true when the patient complains of internal injury that cannot be diagnosed at the EMT level.

An ambulance service is not expected to provide basic
transportation that can be provided equally well by a taxi
or a patient's own automobile. Most third party repayment
plans will not pay an ambulance service unless it is necessary for emergency services, or to provide treatment or
supervision to the patient during transport.

49. Q. **Can a parent refuse to allow treatment to a child in need
of emergency care?**

A. The courts will always overrule the parent and allow treatment if it is necessary to protect or prolong the child's life.

If emergency care is required, the EMT should phone the
police and the ED to take the necessary legal steps to in-
tervene. The EMT, however, should not try to force treatment or transport when both parents refuse consent. If one
parent refuses consent, every effort should be made to get
the consent of the other parent because consent from any
one parent is sufficient.

50. Q. **Is it possible for texts and manuals on emergency care to
be used in a negligence case to show acceptable or current
methods of treatment?**

A. Yes. In the past 10–15 years texts, articles, and instruc-
tional materials from authoritative sources have been used
in court to show acceptable or standard treatment techniques. As with testimony from other EMS personnel, it
helps in defining what others of equal training would do,
or be expected to do in similar circumstances. For example,
the information in this book can be used to show what
should reasonably be expected of EMS personnel.

EMS personnel should carefully read all books and articles relating to emergency care. It will not only keep you
informed of new advances and developments, but give you
a better outlook on what is expected of you.

LEGAL GLOSSARY

accomplice. A person who knowingly, voluntarily, and with common intent with the main offender helps in a crime. As applied to witnesses for the state, and the need for confirming them, "accomplice" includes all persons connected with the offense by an unlawful act or omission either before, at the time of, or after the commission of the offense, whether this witness was present or participated in the crime or not.

action. The legal and formal demand of one's right from another person or party made in a court of justice.

admission. A statement against his or her interest made by a party to an action.

affidavit. A written statement under oath.

amicus curiae. "A friend of the court." An outsider (usually an attorney) who voluntarily appears to file a brief (as *amicus curiae*) and offers information on some matter of law where the judge is doubtful or mistaken, or on a matter of which the court may take judicial recognition.

appeal. A petition to a superior court to review and correct or reverse a possible error committed by a lower court, whose judgment or decision the court above is called upon to correct or reverse.

arbitration. The investigation and determination of a matter or matters of difference between arguing parties by one or more unofficial persons chosen by the parties. These are called arbitrators or referees.

argument. An effort to establish facts by a course of reasoning. For example, the speeches of opposed counsel.

attachment. A proceeding—to take a defendant's property into legal custody to satisfy a plaintiff's legal demand. The object is to hold the property to obey the order of the court for the payment of a judgment in case a defendant must make payment on the debt.

case. A general term for an action, cause, suit, or controversy, at law or in equity. *Case at bar* refers to the particular case which is before the court.

> **prima facie case.** A case which is established by having enough evidence. This case can be overthrown only by denying evidence cited by the other side. (See *rebut.*)

cause. Any question, civil or criminal, challenged before a court of justice.

common law. The common law is that body of law and juristic theory which was originated, developed, and formulated and is admin-

167

istered in England, and has been the law among most of the states and peoples of Anglo-Saxon stock. (See *equity.*)

complaint. In "code states," the complaint is the first or initiatory pleading on the part of the plaintiff in a civil action. It corresponds to the declaration in the common-law practice.

> *cross-complaint.* Whenever the defendant seeks affirmative relief against any party, relating to or depending upon the contract or transaction upon which the action is brought, or affecting the property to which the action relates, he or she may, in addition to his or her answer, file a cross-complaint. Both complaint and cross-complaint contain a statement of the facts, and each demands relief on the facts stated. Each is served upon the opposite party, and each must be answered or other legal pleading must be taken if default judgment is to be avoided.

> *answer.* The formal, written statement under code state provisions, made by a defendant presenting the grounds of his or her defense. It corresponds to what in actions under the common-law practice is called the "plea"; however, as used in a statute providing that the defendant must appear and answer the petition (or declaration). "Answer" refers to any sort of pleading filed by the defendant.

compromise. An arrangement arrived at, either in court or out of court, for settling an argument on what appears to both parties to be equitable terms, considering uncertainty regarding the facts of the law and the facts together. Proof of an offer to compromise the controversy involved in litigation, or the fact that an offer to compromise was made, is generally held not to be permitted as evidence.

conspiracy. A combination or confederacy between two or more persons formed for the purpose of committing, by their joint efforts, some unlawful act or for the purpose of using unlawful means for the commission of an act lawful in itself.

contempt. A willful disregard or disobedience of the court's orders, as well as such conduct that tends to bring the authority of the court and the administration of justice into question.

contract. An agreement, with enough consideration, to do or not to do a certain thing.

> *express contract.* An actual agreement of the parties, the terms of which are openly uttered or declared at the time of making it, stated in distinct and explicit language either orally or in writing.

> *implied contract.* A contract not created or evidenced by the explicit agreement of the parties but implied by law, as a matter of reason and justice from their acts of conduct, the circumstances surrounding the transaction making it a reasonable or even a necessary assumption that a contract existed between

them by clear understanding. For example, contracts in restraint of trade are designed to eliminate or stifle competition, effect a monopoly, artificially maintain prices, or otherwise hamper or obstruct the course of trade and commerce as it would be carried on if left to the control of natural and economic forces. A contract which in its terms is in unreasonable restraint of trade is invalid as against public policy, but a contract in reasonable restraint of trade is valid and enforceable.

contribution. The sharing of a loss or payment among several; a payment made by each or any of several, having a common interest of liability, or his or her share in the loss suffered or money necessarily paid by one in behalf of others. Apart from statute, the general rule is that there can be no contribution between *tortfeasors* (see page **175**) this being against the policy and maxims of the law to adjust equities between wrongdoers, or to allow a person to begin an action on his or her own wrongdoing.

count. In pleading, the different parts of a declaration or complaint, each of which, if it stood alone, would be a ground for action. Count is also used to signify the several parts of an indictment, each charging a distinct offense.

court. An organ of the judicial department of the government whose function is the application of the laws to controversies brought before it and the public administration of justice.

covenant not to sue. An agreement by one who at the time of making it had a right of action against another person, but who agreed not to sue to enforce such right of action.

deposition. Sometimes used equally with oath, but the term is specifically applied to the testimony of a witness taken in writing, under oath or affirmation, before some judicial officer in answer to oral or written questions.

directed verdict. When there is not enough evidence or cause resulting from the evidence which would support a judgment for the one party, the court may, on motion of the other party, direct the jury to bring in a verdict for that other party. (See *verdict*.)

due care. Due or ordinary care means the degree of care which would be exercised by the ordinary careful person in the same circumstances.

equity. It is generally stated that equity is a system administered by a tribunal, other than the established courts, developed because of the inability and, to some degree, the unwillingness of the common law to meet all the requirements of justice. Courts of equity have been called courts of conscience because their object is to deal with legal controversies to allow for full, adequate, and complete justice between the parties in accordance with the dictates of natural justice and good conscience, unhampered by the ritual and stiffness which to some degree limits the power of law courts. (See *common law*.)

error. An error of the court in applying the law to the case on trial. For example, in ruling on the admissibility of evidence or in charging (instructing) the jury.

estoppel. A bar or barrier raised by the law which prevents a person from stating or denying a certain fact or state of facts in consequence of his or her previous statements or denial of conduct or admission, or the result of a final judgment of the matter in a court of law; a person's act or acceptance which stops or closes his or her mouth to state or prove the truth.

ethics. The branch of moral science which deals with the duties a member of a profession owes to the public, to his or her colleagues, and to his or her patients or clients.

evidence. Any type of proof or test of a matter legally presented at the trial of an issue by the parties involved by using witnesses, records, documents, concrete objects, and so forth to influence the minds of the court or jury about their opposition.

> *direct evidence.* When the existence of any fact is proven by witnesses as having come under the awareness of their own senses, or is stated in documents, the genuineness and truth of which there seems no reason to question, the evidence of that fact is said to be direct.

> *circumstantial evidence.* Evidence which suggestively proves the principle fact by establishing a condition of surrounding and limiting circumstances; the existence of the principle fact is only decided by one or more circumstances which have been established directly.

execution. A judicial writ issued by the court when the judgment is made, directed to an officer of the court, and running against the body or goods of a party, by which the judgment of the court is enforced. In general, execution may be issued against any party against whom a judgment may be made, but it cannot be issued against one not a party to the action. Every kind of property or interest not otherwise exempt by statute may be reached by an execution issued on a judgment.

ex parte. An ex parte proceeding is a proceeding by and for one party only, without notice to or opposition by another. It necessarily assumes a right to petition to which there is no opposing party.

felony. A crime of a more serious nature than those known as misdemeanors. In many states felony is defined as any public offense on conviction of which the offender is liable to sentence of death or imprisonment in a penitentiary or state prison; in contrast, misdemeanor is a general name for criminal offenses of every sort which do not in law amount to the grade of felony.

fraud. A standard term which covers the numerous means which can be thought of by the human mind, and carried out by one individual, to gain an advantage over another by false suggestions or by hiding the truth.

garnishment. A legal summons or warning concerning the attachment of property to satisfy a debt. Also, the withholding of a certain sum from wages to satisfy a creditor.

grand jury. A jury that looks at accusations against parties charged with crimes, and if the evidence warrants the jury makes formal charges on which the accused parties are later tried.

hearsay evidence. Evidence not gained from the personal knowledge of a witness but from what the witness has heard other parties say.

indemnify. The process of repaying a party for losses brought on when the obligation to repay under a contractual provision exists.

indemnity. A related contract where one person attempts to protect another person against an anticipated loss.

independent contractor. A person who contracts with another to do something for him or her. This person is not controlled by the other or subject to the other's right to control with respect to his or her physical conduct in the performance of the task.

indictment. An accusation in writing created by a legally summoned and sworn grand jury presented by this jury to the court which it is enrolled in, charging that a person named in the accusation has done some act or been guilty of some omission which, by law, is a public offense punishable on indictment.

inference. A conclusion reached by the jury from the facts proven without an exact direction of law to that effect.

information. An accusation in the nature of an indictment. It is different from an indictment by being presented by a competent public officer on his or her oath of office instead of by a grand jury on their oath.

injunction. A legal action by a court of equity forbidding a party from carrying out a certain action.

instruction by the court. An explanation of the rules or principles of law applicable to some branch or phase of a case, which the jury is bound to accept and apply.

insurance. A contract by which, for a consideration, one party assumes certain risks of another party, and promises to pay the party or his or her nominee a certain or proven sum of money under special circumstances.

invasion of privacy. Interfering on the right of privacy, or the right to be "left alone," to live alone without being subjected to unwarranted or unwanted publicity. Therefore, without the knowledge and permission of the patient, there should be no publication of a medical case record and no showing of a still picture or motion picture from which the identity of a patient can be made.

issue. A single and material point resulting from the allegations of the parties—generally made up of an affirmative and a negative portion.

judgment. The decision or sentence of the law given by a court or other forum resulting from the proceedings of the court or other forum.

> *judgment by default.* Judgment taken against a defendant when, having been summoned or cited in an action, he or she fails to appear at the proper time; a judgment but at the the same time the verdict. In cases where a motion for a directed verdict should have been granted but was denied, the court on its own motion or on the motion of the aggrieved party may pass judgment without the verdict of the jury.

jury. A certain number of persons, selected by law, who are sworn to look into certain matters of fact and to declare the truth upon evidence presented before them.

justice. The constant and permanent administration to give every person his due.

legal duty. An obligation resulting from contract of the parties or the operation of the law.

liability. The state of being bound or obliged in law or justice to do, pay, or make good on something. A legal liability is one where courts of justice recognize and enforce, such as that between opposing parties.

malfeasance. The wrongful or unjust performance of some act which the performer has no right to perform, or which he or she is demanded by contract not to do.

> *misfeasance.* The improper performance of some act which a person may lawfully do.

> *nonfeasance.* The neglect or failure of a person to do some act which he or she should do.

mandamus (Latin, *we command*). A writ issued by a superior court demanding that a certain act or duty be carried out by a governmental body or officer.

mens rea. A guilty mind; a guilty or wrongful purpose; a criminal intent.

moral turpitude. An act of dishonesty, evil, or corruption in the private and social duties which a man owes to his fellow men or to society in general. However, such acts are not immoral in themselves but their illegality lies in the fact of their being positively forbidden by law.

negligence. The omission to do something which a reasonable person, guided by those ordinary considerations which commonly regulate human affairs, would do, or the doing of something which a reasonable and prudent person would not do.

nonsuit. A judgment against the plaintiff when he or she is unable to prove a case, or when he or she refuses or neglects to proceed to the trial of a cause after it has been put in issue. Only a defendant may move for a nonsuit. The directed verdict is a bar to another action but a nonsuit is not.

perjury. Willfully giving, under oath, false testimony important to the issue or point of inquiry in a judicial proceeding or course of justice. Statutes have generally extended the definition to willful false swearing in many different kinds of affidavits and depositions.

police power. The natural power of a government to have reasonable control over people and property in a government's jurisdiction in the interest of the general security, health, safety, morals, and welfare except when it is legally forbidden.

precedent. A ruled case or court decision used to furnish an example or authority for an identical or similar case afterward raising a similar question of law.

preponderance of evidence. Evidence of greater weight or more convincing than the evidence offered in opposition to it.

presumption. A deduction which the law expressly directs be made from certain facts. As an example, there is a presumption that a letter which has been mailed was received by the addressee, but there is no presumption that the letter was mailed.

privileged communication. (1) A communication between parties to a confidential relation so that the receiver cannot be legally forced to reveal it as a witness. For example, a communication between attorney and client, husband and wife, physician and patient, and so forth. (2) A defamatory communication. Making the communication does not expose the party making it to the civil or criminal liability that would follow from it if it was not privileged. These communications may be absolutely privileged, such as statements made by a judge in his or her judicial capacity, or conditionally privileged, such as when a statement is made by one person to another who is in a confidential relation, or who has an interest in the relation. Bad faith with actual spite deprives this type of communication of its privileged character.

privity. Mutual or successive relationship to the same rights of property.

probative. Having the effect of proof; tending to prove or actually proving. (See *proof*.)

proof. The effect of evidence; the establishment of a fact by evidence.

public policy. The principle of law which holds that no subject can lawfully do something which may be injurious to the public or against the public good.

rebut. To rebut is to defeat or take away from the action of something. For example, when a plaintiff in an action produces evidence which raises the possibility of the defendant's liability, and the defendant shows evidence which shows that the presumption is ill-founded, he or she is said to "rebut it."

release. A written contract for which some claim or interest in something is surrendered to another person.

remand. To remand a case brought into an appellate court, or a case removed from one court into another, means to send it back to the court from which it came so that further proceedings in the case, if any, may be taken there.

res ipso loquitor. "The thing speaks for itself." Apparent negligence of common knowledge.

res judicata. A matter decided; a thing judicially acted upon or decided; a thing or matter settled by judgment.

respectable minority rule. Where there is more than one recognized and approved method of treatment applicable to a case, the physician or surgeon is not liable for honest mistakes of judgment in selecting a method. A charge of negligence in a choice of treatment is denied by showing that a respectable minority of expert physicians approved the method selected.

respondent superior. "Let the master answer." This saying means that a master is liable in certain cases for the wrongful acts of his or her servants and is a principal for those of his or her agent.

right. That which a person is entitled to have, or to do, or to receive from others within the limits of the law.

slander. Oral defamation; speaking false words about another resulting in injury to his or her reputation.

stare decisis. "To abide by." The principle that the laws we are governed by should be fixed, definite, and known. When the law is declared by a court of jurisdiction competent to interpret it, such a declaration with no real mistakes or errors is itself evidence of the law until it is changed by competent authority.

stipulation. The term normally given to an agreement made by the attorneys engaged on opposite sides of a cause.

subpoena. A writ or order directed to a person requiring his or her attendance at a particular time and place to testify. It may also require the person to bring any books, documents, or other things under his or her control which he or she is bound by law to produce as evidence (*subpoena duces tecum*).

summons. A writ directed to the sheriff or other proper officer requiring him or her to notify the person named that an action has been started against him or her in the court that the writ came from, and that he or she is required to appear on a day named to answer the complaint in such action.

surety. A person who contracts himself for the payment of a sum of money, or for the performance of something else for another person; a person who, being liable to pay a debt or perform an obligation, is entitled, if it is enforced against him or her, to be repaid by some other person who should have made payment or performed before the surety was compelled to do so.

tort. A legal wrong committed on the person or property of another independent of a contract for which the law gives a civil remedy.

tort-feasor. One who commits or is guilty of a tort. To be "joint tort-feasors," the parties must either act together in committing the wrong, or their acts, if independent of each other, must unite in causing a single injury.

verdict. The final answer given by the jury to the court concerning the matters of fact committed to the jury for their deliberation and determination. (See *directed verdict.*)

will. A written instrument, executed with the formalities of law, whereby a person makes disposition of his property to take effect after his death.

writ. A notice or order, usually issued by a court.

INDEX